Books by the Author

Writing as "Georgia Sallaska"
Three Ships and Three Kings–Novel, Doubleday, 1969
Priam's Daughter–Novel, Doubleday, 1970
The Last Heracles–Novel, Doubleday, 1971

Writing as "G.S. Madden"
The Quest–Motion Picture Novelization, Ace, 1977

Writing as Sasha Miller with Ben Miller
GURPS "Witch World Playbook Supplement"
–Steve Jackson Games, 1989

Writing as Sasha Miller
Falcon Magic–Novel, TOR Publishing, 1994
Ladylord– Novel, TOR Publishing, 1996
Mother Miller's How to Write Good Book,
FoxAcre Press, 1999 & 2002

Writing As Sasha Miller with Andre Norton
To the King a Daughter–Novel, TOR Publishing, 2000
Knight or Knave–Novel, TOR Publishing, 2001
A Crown Disowned–Novel, TOR Publishing, 2002

featuring the ever-popular
Gwendolyn, Stanley and friends
as both Good and Bad Examples

Mother Miller's How To Write Good Book
Copyright ©1999, 2002 Georgia M. Miller
ISBN 0-9709711-5-X
all rights reserved
revised third edition

Press

401 Ethan Allen Avenue
Takoma Park, Maryland 20912 USA
www.foxacre.com

Introduction
by Andre Norton

From the beginning of time, the storyteller has been an important figure in human civilization, for the need to perpetuate information seems inherent in our breed. Before writing was developed, pictures were used for this purpose, as witness the striking art adorning the walls of prehistoric caves. Undoubtedly, many of those illustrations were meant to record great hunts, and tales of such exploits told around a campfire were later painted on rock walls.

Records were next kept on clay slabs, and those tablets have also endured through the millennia. However, the practice of preserving action in illustrations continued. The student has only to examine the friezes and sculptures placed in the temples of Egypt, Sumeria, the Mayan culture, and the half-forgotten land of Khmer to realize that art and writing are very closely akin.

Yes, there have ever been tellers of tales, and they have always sought ways of preserving their works to be handed down to those who followed after. And, though an artist uses colors and a writer words, both creators share a common goal: to foster communication and to share emotions and dreams with others.

In writing, two processes are woven into one. First, the story, which is born of inner talent, must be called forth; then the technique which can shape it into a form that will reveal it to others must be brought to bear upon the raw material. A writer cannot learn talent, for that is an individual gift; but technique, which supplies the method whereby talent may be used in the best possible way, *must* be learned, and learned well. Just as the artist needs to masters the use of color, so the writer must become discriminating in the choice of words. As one follows the wordsmith's trade, this selection becomes second nature, and the author comes to "feel" the proper word instinctively. However, the pattern that will enable these bright bits to be assembled into a meaningful mosaic remains a matter not of intuitive perception but of rational discipline. *Mother Miller's How To Write Good Book* lays out for the beginning word-worker an exact blueprint of the principles of good writing and provides one of the best introductions to the mastery of language-using skills that I have ever seen. Simply and clearly, for any budding author whose imagination is nudging at him or her with a "What?", this wise and whimsical manual, properly applied, will supply the all-important "How."

ANDRE NORTON
Februrary, 2002

Contents

Introduction by Andre Norton 5
Jargon and Abbreviations Used in Ms. Critique: 9
Essay One: Nuts and Bolts 12
Essay Two: Punctuation Or:
    Never Start A Sentence With A Comma 14
Essay Three: Some Punctuational Specifics 18
Essay Four: The Said-Book 36
Through Darkest Mss. With Mother Miller Or:
    Trapping The Wild Said-Bookism 39
Essay Five: Point of View 41
Essay Six: Plots and Non-Plots 47
Essay Seven: Constructing a Plot in Cold Blood 51
Essay Eight: Novel or Short Story? 56
Essay Nine: On Writing Humor 59
Essay Ten: The Write Stuff 61
Essay Eleven: The Eyes Have It 67
Essay Twelve: Building Character 69
Essay Thirteen: Building Bad Character;
    Villains and Other Despicable Beans 78
Essay Fourteen: Criticism and Workshops 80
Recommended Books 86
Essay Fifteen: You Could Always Look It Up 87
Essay Sixteen: Bogeys, Pet Peeves, and Other Stuff 89
Essay Seventeen: Mother Miller's Standard Lectures
    (all-too-frequently used in ms. criticism) 92
Essay Eighteen: A Brief Listing of Grammatical Terms 106
Essay Nineteen: Sit and Set, Lie and Lay 122
Essay Twenty: Clay Feet 123
Principal Parts of Verbs 125
Addendum on Manuscript Style 127
Index 134
About the Author 137

Jargon and Abbreviations Used in Ms. Critique:

POV	stands for Point of View
VPC	stands for View Point Character
MC	stands for Main Character
AU	stands for Author
WW	stands for Wrong Word or, sometimes, Weasel Word
WVT	stands for Wrong Verb Tense
PV	stands for Passive Voice
RC	stands for Reader-Cheater
CL	stands for CLunky Prose

Em-dash means a double hyphen—like this

Ms. is the standard abbreviation for manuscript (singular)

Mss. is the standard abbreviation for manuscripts (plural)

And then there's URP. URP is an excellent, all-purpose technical term, expressing mid-level exasperation with the text in a non-specific and unanalyzed manner. A given URP can be analyzed as to what constitutes the URP-factor, of course, and if and/or when the discussion gets to the real nuts-and-bolts stage, it is, frequently at agonizing length and thoroughness.

(A milder form of URP is expressed by YUK. URP is related to YUK, only farther down the scale toward S**T. [Or *HI*.] Both S**T and *HI* are useful in ms. critique, depending on how forcefully the critic wishes to express herself.) *Urg* and *oof* and *sigh* and other similar comments apply as the occasion demands.

English sorely lacks a non-gender-specific third person singular pronoun. English is also a thoroughly sexist language—something that is not smiled on today, and high time, though such sexism is virtually invisible thanks to our having seen it all our lives and not being able to recognize it as a result. Throughout this work, Mother Miller will use the feminine or masculine pronouns at random where Gentle Reader may expect all to be the so-called Genderless Male pronoun. The distribution of these pronouns will be masculine or feminine solely at Mother Miller's discretion and/or whim. Get used to it. It's part of her weird allure.

Mother Miller intensely dislikes and only reluctantly will use constructions that involve the use of the excellent non-gender-specific third person plural pronouns (they, their, themselves, etc.) to refer to third person singular. "A writer must attend to its craft" strikes her as an inadequate solution to the non-gender-specific question. And she flatly refuses to refer to all writers as masculine, which is as offensive as referring to all writers as feminine. She hopes that this oddity of hers will become familiar if not invisible as Gentle Reader progresses through the pages, and that Gentle Reader will accept it as just one more of Mother Miller's many charming—if a teensy bit cranky—little quirks and crochets. Gentle Reader doesn't have to love it—only to accept it as an effort to raise Gentle Reader's consciousness on the pervasiveness of sexist language among us.

Gentle Reader, being both an observant sort and above average in brightness (at least bright enough to be reading this book), will also notice that examples here and there throughout are set in a different typeface. Courier is the weapon of choice for ms. preparation, and so, for clarity and visual impact, this is how examples appear if they are items that will appear in a ms.

Some people prefer a sans-serif typeface, such as

12 pt. Arial

but I don't care for it as being hard to read plus being proportional. The eye is more accustomed to serif fonts—the ones with the little twiddly bits added top and bottom—and that's a fact. If I have problems with it, I figure somebody else will, too. Better safe, as they say, than sorry.

Essay One:
Nuts and Bolts

The emphasis in this work is on the technical aspects of writing—the nuts and bolts. This is the punctuation, the grammar, the microwriting.

Microwriting is the way words are put together to convey what the writer has in mind instead of their going astray and winding up as something altogether different and sometimes—too often, actually—unintentionally hilarious.

If a good (i.e. competent in the technical sense) ms.'s purpose is to provide adequate traffic signs to guide the reader toward a close semblance of the story the writer has conceived in her mind, the sloppy techniques one runs into too often these days scuttle the whole project. Writers lazily have their characters shrugging or sitting or grinning dialogue, they indulge in wildly incorrect punctuation and shabby grammar where sentences (yea, entire paragraphs) make no logical sense and sometimes say the opposite of what the author (presumably) intended, and otherwise clutter up the landscape with billboards and political posters from two campaigns ago. The reader either has to fight her way through the unnecessary verbal underbrush or close the book quietly and go away, never to return. This is something every writer has to learn—that he is not in charge. The reader has the ultimate power.

All I can teach is technical competence—to help the writer transmit the story that's in her head onto the paper in a clear enough form that the reader has a shot at re-creating a close approximation of it in *his* head as well. If there's no story to begin with, that pretty much writes paid to the whole effort.

It trots in tandem. Those who work with words must hone and refine their skills constantly so they can to transfer that wonderful story that has taken shape in their heads onto the page clearly enough that it has a hope of being re-created in the head of the reader and have it survive this process as intact as possible. To accomplish this miracle, these language skills must be integrated into a writer's very bones so they become tools of her trade, and not self-conscious techniques.

All it takes to see this too clearly in action is to have a quick read through a few amateur mss. to see why some amateurs are likely to remain so. One of the quickest ways to get a ms. rejected, and never mind the story the ms. is trying to relay, is poor handling of our mother tongue. Adverbial clauses, dangling participles, and other atrocities abound and scream "Amateur Hour"!

One of the big things an acquiring editor looks at is how much work she will have to put into a ms. to make it publishable. Think about it. You turn in a messy ms., you are, in effect, shooting yourself in the foot before you ever get off the ground, if you don't mind a mangled metaphor. If your ms. is *really* a grammatical horror show, you won't even get far enough with an editor for him to find out if the story is decent.

To be fair, grammatical law-breaking is not usually a calculated assault on the rules of the language. Rather, this represents mistakes of ignorance.

Whether we like it or not, whether we think it is "fair" or not, grammar and punctuation do have rules, and they are rules we must learn, each and every one of us, and furthermore, they are rules that must be followed. Yes, there is a little latitude, but precious little. You don't want to hurl your reader out of the dream by some mistake that is easily corrected if only you had known how to do it.

That's what grammar, punctuation, etc. is all about. If a would-be writer thinks learning all this is just too boring for words and doesn't want to bother with it, then Mother Miller strongly suggests he ought to sit down and seriously re-think his ambitions along these lines.

Essay Two:
Punctuation
Or:
Never Start A Sentence With A Comma

Punctuation exists to create a series of guideposts designed to help the reader find her way among the words, in hopes that by setting up these guideposts the author can persuade the reader to perceive something similar to the story the author set out to tell.
    Without the proper punctuation, in a sentence like

```
"He put on the gray fur lined mittens and
slung the brown skinned pack over his
shoulder. . ."
```

the reader is all at sea about whether the mittens or the fur is gray, whether the pack is brown or has just been skinned and is now brown—or anything else that is going on. Readers—not to mention editors—don't like playing mystery games like this, and will set the work aside at once.
    When dealing with compound adjectives, as above, the mnemonic is to separate the two adjectives and see if they can stand alone. If they can't, hyphenate them. Thus, one may have a brown pack but not, logically, a skinned pack. One therefore has a brown-skinned pack and that's wrong also because the pack is made of skin instead of having been skinned. This sloppy syntax, by the way, was taken directly from a writing student's ms. and Mother Miller certainly hopes Gentle Reader does not think she composed it all by herself.

```
a plain brown wrapper

a poison-laced cucumber sandwich
```

It is a convention in this country to put the quotation mark after the period or comma. This dates back to the days when type was set by hand, and doing it otherwise allowed the quote mark to slip down out of place. We carry the tradition on today although some of the strictness is loosening. If there is non-dialogue, quoted material in the text that has nothing to do with a subsequent comma or semicolon, the punctuation can go outside the quote mark and the world will continue to wag.

In this country, the single quotation mark is used only inside the double quote mark, to indicate a quotation within a quotation. Any other usage is incorrect. Mother Miller has noted a distressing tendency for people to try to use single quotes for material that is not dialogue. This is wrong. All quoted material, whether dialogue or not, goes in double quotes; single quote marks are reserved for quotes contained therein. This is not negotiable.

There are two spaces after the end of a sentence, and two spaces after a colon. This calls attention to the end of the sentence and helps keep the colon from being mistaken for a semi-colon. It also is vital in doing printer's word counts, which is different from ms. word counts, being based on en-spaces, a given number of which constitute a "printer's word". There is a growing preference for one space at the end of a sentence, but I defiantly remain Unreconstructed in this regard. Two spaces I use, resisting the fad, and ever will.

Punctuation in dialogue causes a lot of problems.

```
"Meet me in the gazebo." Gwendolyn said.
```

This is wrong. "Meet me in the gazebo" is not a complete sentence because it is connected to "Gwendolyn said." If it stood alone, the period would be fine. You must use a comma.

```
"I am consumed with delight," Stanley
```

```
said, "I'll meet you at half-past six."
```

This is wrong because Stanley has spoken two complete sentences and they cannot be joined by a comma. The "logical" spot for the period (after the word delight) is already occupied by another conventional usage, the comma. Therefore, the only other spot for it is after "said."

```
        "If I am late," Stanley said, "Start
without me."
```

The capital S is wrong because it is in the middle of a line of dialogue that is a single complete sentence, interrupted by "Stanley said,". Use a lower-case S.

```
        "If I am late," Stanley scampered
playfully from the gazebo, "start without me."
```

To be correct, a line of dialogue can be interrupted only by a vocality-phrase like "he said", "she muttered", etc. Action-phrases, or, as they are sometimes called, business-phrases, must utilize dashes instead:

```
        "If I am late—" Stanley scampered
playfully from the gazebo "—start without me."
```

Both dashes go inside the quotation marks, taking the place of the comma, question mark, etc. Em-dashes conventionally indicate an interruption in speech, and this is a convention that indicates the taking up again of the interrupted speech when done by the original speaker. Doing it the "logical" way would leave the end word in the action phrase (in this case, "gazebo") without any punctuation of its own.

A hyphen is a hyphen. It is not a dash. For dashes, use two hyphens—like this—without any spaces around them. This is called an em-dash, and must be marked for the typesetter. If the author includes spaces fore and aft as well — like this — they must be deleted, by hand, each and every one. It costs so little to gain a few points by making some poor copyeditor's life easier. *The Chicago Manual of Style* uses this convention and if it's good enough for them, rest assured it's good enough for the rest of us.

Mother Miller too often runs across places in mss. where the author, apparently despairing of her ability to get the point across any other way, resorts to stacked punctuation, like this!! Or this !?!?! Don't commit this error. If your prose isn't strong enough to begin with, no amount of excess punctuation, is going to salvage it.

Essay Three:
Some Punctuational Specifics

The Period

The period is used to mark the end of a declarative sentence, and is followed by two spaces.

>   Gwendolyn was moping in the gazebo.
>   Stanley was over an hour late.

The period also comes after most abbreviations, in which case it is followed by a single space (to set it off from a sentence end).

>   Ms. Gwendolyn Goodnyss, Mr. Stanley Wanderlust

The period follows after numerals or letters in a vertical list, followed by a single space.

>   1. chocolate bon-bons
>   2. lace pillows
>   a. cufflinks
>   b. tie clip

Do not use a period at the end of a sentence that is incorporated within another sentence.

>   Stanley's usual excuse, "I was tied up in traffic," was beginning to wear very thin.

Periods belong inside brackets or parentheses if the parenthetical matter is an independent sentence; otherwise they go outside.

>   Gwendolyn, heart a-throb (and about to
> burst the stays on her second-best corset),
> recognized Stanley's footsteps. (Stanley had
> recently purchased new shoes, which tended to
> squeak.)
>
>   Gwendolyn stood moping at the entrance to
> the gazebo (she could scarcely believe how
> late Stanley was) as she petulantly shook her
> diamond wrist-watch, certain that it must have
> stopped.

The Question Mark

The question mark is used after a direct question.

>   "Where have you been, Stanley?" Gwendolyn
> cried tranquilly.

The question mark does not end a request or order, even though it has been politely phrased as a question.

>   "Will you kindly stop nagging and hold
> your peace."

The question mark also does not end an indirect question.

>   Gwendolyn asked herself if she had heard
> Stanley correctly.

The Exclamation Point

The exclamation point is used to create a little excitement after an exclamatory word, phrase, or sentence, and sometimes after an ironical comment.

>   "What a surprise!" she said. "I had

thought you dead ere now."

"I nearly was!" Stanley said, surprised. "The traffic was terrible!"

"Another big surprise! The traffic."

Judicious use of the exclamation point and also the occasional Said-Bookism (see section titled The Said-Book for more on this) clears up possible misunderstandings:

"Fire," Stanley said.

"Fire!" Stanley shouted.

Be chary of using too many exclamation points, as they tend to bludgeon a reader into insensibility. Here, as elsewhere, less really is more.

The Comma

The comma is probably the most misused piece of punctuation in the entire language. First, the comma is used between independent clauses of equal value that are short and incorporate no commas within them (in which case the semi-colon comes into use).

Gwendolyn did needlepoint, she loved fine lace undergarments, and she spent a great deal of time in the gazebo waiting for Stanley.

A comma comes between two independent clauses that are joined by coordinating or correlative conjunctions (examples: *and, but, or, nor, neither, yet, for, so*).

Gwendolyn had not seen the fire yet, so she had no idea what to do to remedy the situation.

Stanley gestured frantically, but could

not make her understand.

>Gwendolyn had now discovered the fire, yet she was reluctant to act.

A comma is needed (for clarity) after a dependent clause, usually a lengthy one, that comes before an independent clause.

>When it became apparent that Stanley was unable or perhaps unwilling to do something about the fire, Gwendolyn made her decision.

Two or more verbs having the same subject (known as a compound predicate) should not be separated by a comma.

>She reached over and picked up the pitcher of lemonade.

If the predicate is not compound—if the two actions are not logically related—then do separate them with a comma.

>"Lemonade is quite refreshing at times," she said, and smiled.

Commas set off the one or ones spoken to in direct address.

>"Come here, Stanley, and bend over," Gwendolyn said tersely.

Appositives (the words following a noun or pronoun which identify it) are set off by commas, if they are nonrestrictive. These words add parenthetical information without being further set off by parentheses.

>Stanley Wanderlust, bon vivant and Tiddledewinks champion, hastened to obey.

If the appositive is restrictive, omit the commas.

> Gwendolyn the pure of heart gritted her teeth in anticipation of the task confronting her.

Use a comma between two adjectives when they modify the same noun and the word "and" could be used between them without altering the meaning.

> She raised the cool, frosty pitcher of lemonade and took deadly aim.

If the first adjective modifies the idea set forth by the second adjective and noun combined, no comma is used to separate the adjectives.

> Her creamy Southern complexion reddened a trifle with her blushes and the unaccustomed exertion.

An adverbial phrase beginning a sentence is usually followed by a comma.

> By pouring the lemonade on the seat of Stanley's trousers, she could put out the fire.

An adverbial phrase that occurs between the subject and the verb in a sentence is set off by commas.

> Stanley, before allowing his beloved to extinguish him, turned to throw her one last kiss.

The comma may be omitted after very short introductory adverbial phrases.

> As one they realized what must be done to save Stanley's life and even his manhood.

A comma is not used after an introductory adverbial phrase immediately preceding the verb it modifies.

> Out of the bushes beside the gazebo popped Gwendolyn's father.

A restrictive dependent clause (one that would alter the meaning of the main clause if omitted) following a main clause should not be set off by a comma. A nonrestrictive clause in the same position is preceded by a comma.

> Mr. Goodnyss would extinguish the fire if Gwendolyn would get out of the way.

> She agreed to step aside, though she was a little piqued at his interference.

Commas set off nonrestrictive phrases and nonrestrictive clauses that give descriptive information not essential to the meaning of the sentence.

> Mr. Goodnyss, who secretly wished Stanley would perish in the conflagration, languidly lifted the garden hose.

No comma is used with a restrictive, or essential clause.

> The man whose pants were on fire could not have cared less about his rescuer's personal opinion of him.

A dependent clause coming before the main clause should usually be set off by a comma regardless of whether it is restrictive or nonrestrictive.

> If Stanley should char, Gwendolyn knew her life would be much more sedate.

An introductory participial or infinitive phrase should be set off by a comma unless it immediately precedes (and forms part of) the verb.

```
    Moving to the table, Gwendolyn moodily
surveyed the spectacle confronting her.

    To obey her father, she would have to
sacrifice her beloved.
```

A comma sets off absolute phrases—i.e., phrases composed of a noun or pronoun plus a participle that are not joined to the rest of the sentence by relationship words.

```
    Her mind made up, she tightened her grasp
on the forgotten pitcher of lemonade.
```

Commas set off a parenthetical clause, phrase, or word that is logically close to the rest of the sentence. Two commas. One fore, one aft. Parenthetical elements that are less logically related to the rest of the sentence need to be set off by dashes, or by parentheses.

```
    The courageous maiden hefted the pitcher
and knew, in the depths of her love-smitten
heart, that the contents had grown tepid.

    This mattered not for she realized—clever
little minx that she was—the opportunity
before her.
```

A comma follows the exclamatory oh but not the vocative O.

```
    Oh, my dear father! O despot of the
family!
```

Use commas to set off interjections, transitional adverbs, and other expressions that cause a break in the flow of thought.

```
    Well, it had to be done.

    It was, after all, the only action
remaining to her since her father was dawdling
about so long with the hose.
```

Two or more complementary (antithetical) phrases referring to a single word following them should be set off by commas from each other and from the words following.

```
    His brawny, though inconveniently fragile,
hands seemed unable to adjust the nozzle
satisfactorily.
```

An antithetical phrase or clause starting with "not" should be set off by commas if it is unessential to the meaning of the modified element.

```
    Strangely enough her father, not the man
whose pants were on fire, presented the more
immediate problem.
```

Interdependent antithetical clauses are set off by a comma. Short ones, however, are not.

```
    The longer she waited, the greater the
emergency would become.

    The sooner the better.
```

Three or more elements in a series are separated by commas. When the last two elements (words, phrases, clauses) are joined by a conjunction, the comma comes before the conjunction.

```
    Gwendolyn's countenance radiated love,
trust, innocence, and just a small touch of
greed.
```

When elements in a series are very simple and are all joined by conjunctions, no commas are used.

>   She was by turns complicated and reckless
>   and silly.

When a series ends with "etc." in the middle of a sentence, a comma follows the "etc."

>   Stanley had frequently complained about
>   her extravagance, her figure, her credulity,
>   etc., while at the same time praising her
>   punctuality.

A comma is used after such terms as *that is, i.e., e.g.*, and *namely* when they are used to introduce a series or an example.

>   She realized her problem anew, namely,
>   that she wished her father absent while
>   simultaneously desiring that Stanley's fire
>   was put out.

Sometimes a comma must be inserted to keep the meaning clear.

>   To Gwendolyn, Stanley was an ideal,
>   friend, and critic.

Two identical words should be separated by a comma to make reading easier.

>   When she moped in the gazebo, he often
>   came in, in a foul humor himself.

A comma is used to set off conjunctive adverbs (such as however, moreover) and transitional adverbs.

>   She despised his moodiness; moreover, she
>   felt it interfered with her own.

A comma is not used with an indirect quote.

```
Stanley always said she loved to be the
center of attention.
```

Do not carelessly link two main clauses with only a comma between them (comma splice), or, worse, without any punctuation at all (fused sentence).

The Semi-Colon

The semi-colon is used in compound sentences between independent clauses not joined by connectives, particularly if they are extended or have commas within them. The comma alone is not strong enough to do the job; therefore, the semi-colon finds its place in the world. Think of it as epoxy holding the two clauses together; the comma and the half of the colon make up the two parts of the epoxy compound.

```
Oh, she loathed them both; she wished they
would leave her alone in her precious gazebo,
though if either of them brought her fresh ice
for her lemonade she would not object.
```

A semi-colon punctuates the elements in a series for which further division than that provided by commas is needed.

```
She didn't know whether Stanley had been
born in Paris, France; Paris, Texas; or
Tuscaloosa, Alabama.
```

The Colon

The colon is one of the most overused—and inappropriately used—pieces of punctuation in the English language. It is far too powerful, and too formal, for most storytelling. Writers who are shaky with punctuation will sometimes throw in a few colons, in what appears to be an attempt to bluff their way through a sticky situation by giving it that high-tech look. Properly, the colon is used to stress the connection between two clauses that form a single sentence or to separate one clause from a second clause that illustrates or amplifies the first. A good thing to keep in mind is that the colon is a mighty tool, the single most shocking punctuation mark there is, more powerful than a period or exclamation mark, and as such is magnitudes of order too powerful for use in writing fiction. Use the colon sparingly, if at all, and always with exquisite correctness.

A colon is used to introduce a part of a sentence that exemplifies, restates, or explains the preceding part.

```
     Many of Stanley's traits puzzled her: some
of these little quirks, in fact, could only
have been the result of an unhappy childhood.
```

The colon is used to introduce a series or list.

```
     Stanley had only three present complaints
about Mr. Goodnyss: his miserliness, his
ubiquity, and his ineptness with the nozzle on
the hose.
```

If the list or series comes after such an expression as *namely, for instance, for example*, or *that is*, a colon is correct only if the series consists of one or more grammatically complete clauses.

```
     His ordinary complaints were more general,
namely, his stupidity, his smelly socks, and
his lack of common sense.

     For example: Mr. Goodnyss was still trying
to figure out the trigger on the garden hose
nozzle; the odor of his smelly socks was
threatening to overpower the smell of
Stanley's woolen trousers burning; and Mr.
Goodnyss had not paid the water bill recently.
```

The terms *as follows* and *the following* require a colon if followed immediately by the illustrations or listed items, or if the introducing clause is incomplete without such items.

> Gwendolyn solved many of her problems as follows: she dashed a portion of the lemonade into her father's face, used the rest to put out the fire on Stanley's trousers, tied up her father with the garden hose and eloped with a grateful Stanley who asked her to marry him as soon as the fire was out.

A colon is also used to introduce an extended quotation.

The Hyphen

In manuscript preparation, if you are smart, you will never, ever leave hyphenated words at the end of the line—it confuses the daylights out of typesetters, who don't know what to do with these hyphens. Also, each of these has to be marked and you don't want to give anyone an excuse to come at your work with a marking implement. Even compound words (such as mother-in-law) should not be broken at the end of the line, for the same reason. Go ahead and leave that big gap at the right margin. It's quite all right to do so.

A hyphen connects the parts of some compound words used as nouns or adjectives. It is also used in some words formed with prefixes.

> an all-out attack, a rosy-cheeked cherub, a well-known but ill-favored troubadour who was a ne'er-do-well at heart

A hyphen is not used when a compound adjective comes after the noun or when the first word is an adverb ending in -ly.

> The attack was well planned.
> The badly planned counter-attack was poorly received.

A hyphen joins compound numbers from twenty-one to ninety-nine, and is used to express fractions, though the fraction should not be hyphenated if one element already has a hyphen.

```
    Stanley was twenty-six years old.

    Gwendolyn had one three-quarters full
glass of lemonade liberally laced with vodka
to brace herself for the ordeal with the
shabbily dressed justice of the peace.
```

Neither "liberally laced" nor "shabbily dressed" take a hyphen because both "liberally" and "shabbily" are adverbs acting like adjectives (modifying "laced" and "dressed", respectively) that come before the noun. Also, they look like compound adjectives, which just makes matters worse somehow.

The Dash

The dash shows a break in continuity or thought in a sentence. The convention is to use a dash to indicate an abrupt interruption, and an ellipse to indicate a thought or speech trailing off into nothing.

```
    That night, as Stanley and Gwendolyn slept
together for the first time—where was she,
anyway?
```

The dash—not the colon, as happens far too frequently—is used to emphasize an appositive.

```
    Gwendolyn was more than his beloved—she
was his way out of the gazebo and Mr.
Goodnyss's range of vision.

    Oh, Gwendolyn, my turtledove—my tax
deduction—why didn't you tell me you suffered
from somnambulism?
```

A dash sets off parenthetical material resulting from a break in thought or continuity.

> Gwendolyn walked along the roof of the building—how delicately she trod!—coming perilously closer to the edge with every step she took.

Multiple Punctuation

When two different punctuation marks are called for at the same point in a sentence, the stronger of the two wins, and the other is dropped.

> "Gwendolyn, can't you watch where you're going?" Stanley screeched.

More On Quotation Marks

Quotation marks enclose direct quotations and dialogue. A new paragraph indicates a change in speaker; for this reason, paragraph changes within a single long speech startle and confuse readers. This is where "business-phrases" come in. The speaker or the listener breaks the long speech instead; this is a good time for Gwendolyn to twist a lock of her hair, or for Stanley to pick at his cuticles. Someone can stare thoughtfully out the window, or they can gaze soulfully into each other's eyes. Or the listener can say,

> "Huh? I didn't quite get that last—"

Whatever it takes to break up a long, long speech without also snapping the reader's concentration.

Always be careful to put action- or business-phrases with the one who is doing the action. If the next speech is by that same character, put the speech in the same paragraph as well.

For quoted passages of one hundred or more words, indent and single-space the quotation and do not enclose it in quotation marks. This rule is for the outside world, however, and is not used in ms. preparation. Keep it double-spaced throughout.

Parentheses

Use parentheses sparingly in storytelling. Parenthetical material is, almost by definition, something that is not read. Most often, parentheses indicate a sloppy, poorly constructed sentence that needs to be re-written. Properly, parentheses are used to enclose very loosely (if at all) related comments, side remarks, explanations, etc., and many readers, sometimes including Mother Miller, simply skip past them. Use em-dashes to enclose parenthetical information without having to resort to parentheses.

Ellipses

Three spaced dots stand for an omission within or at the beginning of a sentence.

```
     There had been a note on the Formica top
of Gwendolyn's nightstand, written in a hasty
but ladylike scrawl using a piece of mint-
flavored chocolate! Stanley searched
feverishly only to find that he had licked
away all but the last two lines on the
surface: ". . . my dearest love. Sincerely,
Gwendolyn."
```

Four dots (a period followed by three spaced dots) are used as an ellipsis that ends a sentence.

```
     "Ah, alas and alack," Stanley said
mournfully. "If only I had wakened earlier. .
. ."
```

The fourth dot takes the place of the missing period.

The Apostrophe

The apostrophe indicates the possessive case (except for personal pronouns), to mark omissions, and to form the plurals of letters and figures. If there is ambiguity created by using an apostrophe in, say, an acronym (NASA's paperwork is enormous for the work it does which is why there are no more NASA's around than there are already), then omit the apostrophe in favor of clarity.

If the ending (either singular or plural) is not an *s* or *z* sound, add the apostrophe and *s*.

```
the man's hat, the boy's coat, today's
news (singular)

the men's hats, the children's dog,
women's dresses (plural)

one's hat, another's coat, someone's belt
(indefinite pronouns, singular)
```

If the plural ends in an *s* or *z* sound, add only the apostrophe.

```
ladies' handbags, boys' shoes, the
Joneses' butler, ten dollars' worth of bonbons
```

If the singular ends in an *s* or *z* sound, add the apostrophe and *s* for words of one syllable. Add only the apostrophe for words of more than one syllable unless you expect the pronunciation of the second *s* or *z* sound.

```
James's books, Moses' law, Xerxes' army,
Hortense's coat
```

Compounds or nouns in joint possession show the possessive in the last word only. But if there is individual (or separate) possession, each noun takes the possessive form.

```
My brother-in-law's house; my brothers-in-
law's houses, someone else's hat.

Stanley and Gwendolyn's automobile (joint
ownership)

Stanley's and Gwendolyn's toothbrushes
(separate ownership)
```

Do not use the apostrophe with the pronouns his, hers, its, ours, yours, theirs, whose or with plural nouns not in the possessive case.

```
WRONG: hi's pony; it's nest; a friend of
your's and their's; who's mistake; who'se
mistake

RIGHT: his pony; its nest; a friend of
yours and theirs; whose mistake

WRONG: He makes hat's for ladies'.

RIGHT: He makes hats for ladies.
```

Use an apostrophe to mark omissions in contracted words or numerals.

```
Can't, didn't, he's (he is), it's (it is),
you're (you are), o'clock (of the clock), the
class of '89
```

Use the apostrophe and *s* to form the plural of letters, figures, symbols and words referred to as words.

```
Gwendolyn seldom crossed her t's, her 7's
looked like 9's, and her and's were usually
&'s.
```

Writers who are shaky on points of grammar, sentence construction, and punctuation would be well advised to study on their own, following rules slavishly, if necessary. Relying on someone else—even Mother Miller—to insert necessary commas, delete unnecessary ones, re-parse sentences, correct grammar and syntax errors, etc., teaches little, develops no understanding. Knowing what is required in a particular situation is a big step along the way toward mastery of that most basic of all writing tools, the English language.

And airy statements about how rules are for breaking don't cut much ice with Mother Miller, either, who comes down firmly on the side of the point of view that states one must know the rules first so that one can break them successfully later.

Essay Four:
The Said-Book

The verb "to say," contrary to what some writers apparently believe, has only the standard number of forms. It's the substitutes for "to say" that make up what writers who strive for purity in the language call the Said-Book.

Said-Bookisms are artificial, literary verbs used to avoid the perfectly good word "said." "Said" is one of the few invisible words in the language; it acts as "white noise" for the eyes and is almost impossible to overuse. And it is infinitely less distracting than "he retorted," "she inquired," or the all-time favorite, "he ejaculated." "He answered" also finds itself on some people's proscribed list; if someone asks a question, and someone else says something in return, of course "he answered" or "he replied." It is implicit in the text. If a writer gets tired of "he said", he can always eliminate the vocal tag altogether. Some of the most sparkling dialogue is written in just this fashion.

Probably the most cogent objection to the Said-Book is that it is, ultimately, a lazy way to write. One can say, *"Stop that," she spat*, and not have to go to all the trouble and bother of setting up the character's frame of mind or the mood she's in. It's so much easier just to say, *"Thank you," he condescended*, than to convey the situation the hard way, through character exposition. It is also a prime signal for a knowing reader to set the work aside; after all, if an author cannot be trusted not to take the easy way out in these little things, he can't be trusted not to take short-cuts on larger issues, such as plot points.

The Said-Book also functions as a kind of Countersinking (see Standard Lectures) and in any case demonstrates that the writer is either not trusting her own words, or isn't trusting the reader to figure out what is really going on without being hammered over the head repeatedly. Please, run out right now and buy a smaller hammer so you can set the Said-Book aside.

Some beginning (and, alas, some not-so-new) writers get confused about vocal tags and think non-verbal gestures are synonyms for "said." Their characters shrug, wave, wink, and generally do everything but talk.

Vocalities other than "say" or "ask" can be just as annoying. Writers who let their characters bark, snarl, etc., do themselves and their readers a disservice. When the writer needs something stronger than "said" ("'Fire!' Stanley said" just doesn't adequately convey the message), he has nowhere to go, since he escalated the situation so sharply from the beginning.

Some examples:

```
"Come here, kitty," Gwendolyn hissed.
```

Not only does this speech not contain any sibilants to be hissed, but also it leaves the reader wondering, bewildered, if Gwendolyn has turned into a serpent.

```
"Get lost, cat," Stanley shrugged.
```

A shrug is accomplished by a movement of the shoulders. Speech is accomplished with the tongue, lips, teeth and larynx. Stanley may say this while shrugging, but that's about it.

```
"Go to the window," Stanley sat down at
the table, "and throw out the cat."
```

Oddly enough, an interjection in a speech, like this one, can be mended with the proper modern punctuation:

```
"Go to the window—" Stanley sat down at
the table "—and throw out the cat."
```

```
"Meow," the cat grinned.
```

Not even the famous Cheshire Cat could pull this one off. Grin "Hello" as an exercise, and see how far it gets you. Do the same exercise with wink and shrug and giggle and laugh and all those other quaint non-vocal verbs you are tempted to use in dialogue, as well.

Throw the Said-Book out the window, instead of the cat, and reserve a judicious few for use at times when maximum impact is required and the situation is such that a simple "he said" just won't carry the burden. If an author is in doubt, a useful exercise is to substitute for the Said-Bookism another, even worse nonsense word, such as *cardboarded* or *windowpaned* or *rainstormed* or—Mother Miller's own litmus test, *garbaged*— for the one the author originally had in mind. If it still stands up under this, and if the Said-Bookism really does do its small job of adding to the story instead of trying to do a major job of carrying the mood, use it with Mother Miller's blessing.

Then go right back to "said" when you use a vocal tag at all.

Through Darkest Mss. With Mother Miller Or: Trapping The Wild Said-Bookism

Mother Miller has come across more than her share of truly odd and awful Said-Bookisms in her time of working with writers. Cut, sliced, clipped, crushed, and many, many more verbs new writers have written, thinking they were injecting sparkle into the story, have cluttered up ms. pages. Just when she thinks she has surely seen it all, a new one comes along. Moodily, she has begun keeping a list.

"You do that so well," he admired.

"Oh, thank you," she farted wistfully.

"And one thing more," he chimed.

"This is the last thing I have to say," he climaxed.

"This is all I can take," he swallowed.

"Bah," he literally hum-bugged.

"Is that so?" she mocked a retort.

"Oh, come now," he condescended.

"Now see here," he throttled.

"What is it this time?" he rolled.

"Open this door at once," he pounded, "and let me in!"

"Oh, very well," she capitulated.

"Power!" he delivered, rising from his chair.

"I love you," he ejaculated.

"What a pretty girl," he complimented.

"No, I won't," she denied him.

"I'll see you dead," he menaced.

"I don't think so," she muffled through her cloak.

And the list goes on. . . .

Essay Five:
Point of View

Through whose eyes are you seeing the scene unfolding? That's the Point of View.

The technical term for the most widely accepted and used modern POV technique is *third person omniscient.* The story is told by an unnamed narrator (a persona of the author) who can dip into the mind and thoughts of any character, though he focuses primarily on no more than two or three. This gives the writer the greatest range and freedom. The narrator can speak in her own voice, filling in necessary background or offering objective observations; yet when the scene is intense and her presence would be intrusive, she can slip into third-person limited POV, thus vanishing from the reader's consciousness.

Third person omniscient POV is the most versatile, and by extension, the easiest on both reader and author. The reader doesn't have to work so hard at remembering through whose consciousness he is receiving the story, and the author may switch scenes (and consciousnesses) when he wishes to explore some information the previous viewpoint character (VPC) had no access to or any right to know. In other words, this way, the reader is in on the whole plot—frequently knows more about the situation than does the Hero—and thus is even more deeply involved when the Hero goes blundering into the morass the reader knows about and the Hero doesn't. Making the reader feel quite smart is quite smart on the author's part, every single time. And that's a promise.

The writer isn't playing fair when he begins to write in third person[s] limited POV—i.e., viewing the landscape through more than one set of eyes per scene. "Limited" means just that—both author and reader are constrained to one set of perceptions for that scene.

No matter how good Gwendolyn is at it, she can't report reliably what Stanley is seeing or thinking; she can report only what she sees or hears. Next scene, Stanley can see and/or think for himself—and his perceptions may be altogether different from hers.

There's nothing inherently wrong with using multiple viewpoints; the trick is for the author to restrain himself to doing them one at a time—one per scene, or one per segment, or one per chapter, or whatever. That way the reader can get her bearings, settle into this head, and get on with the story. In many cases, such as when the reader finally gets a peek inside the head of the arch-villain, this comes as a welcome shift, as information avidly sought, and as a greater hook into the story itself. Timing, here as in various other pursuits, is all.

At its most basic, a reader is entitled to the courtesy of having a single head at a time to occupy—a single, well, Point Of View. It does create some technical difficulties when you, the author, wish to give me, the reader, more information than I'm entitled to have, such as what the other guy is thinking in response to what the scene VPC has said or done. However, that's why there are amateur writers and professionals. If you want to progress from amateur status to profession you'll stick with one POV per scene, please, and if you've used up your quota, you have to shift scenes.

Mother Miller has come to the opinion that a lot of the difficulty she sees in POV is due to that well-known and quite popular whipping boy, television. In a television drama, there is no designated POV. Furthermore, as the camera switches within a scene so, perforce, does the onlooker's POV. This may be all well and good in television or even movies, but it is not—repeat, not—good regards the written word.

The convention is that the first character in a given scene is the one the reader can expect to be the VPC for that scene. The reader gets testy, often without realizing it, if he gets fooled on that score, and begins to mutter to himself and shift about in his chair. Why can't this writer stick to giving me one person's viewpoint at a time? she thinks. I just get comfortable inside one skull and *bip!* I'm knocked into another. Makes me feel like a sparrow that got caught in the badminton game. Then the reader sets the book aside, goes and gets an aspirin, and never returns.

POV shifting within a scene is, therefore, against the law because it causes extreme vertigo in the reader who doesn't know where he is, or with whom he is supposed to identify at any given moment. It is also a copout for the author, who then doesn't have to bother with boring technical details such as structured plotting, as she can blab all by simply tapping in on whomever it is convenient to do so, any time he wishes—which technique is called *authorial omniscient*. All knowing and all telling, too often.

Authorial omniscient can be handled well, the trouble being it so seldom is. For a while authorial-omniscient viewpoint—calm, wise, all knowing, non-judging—was in great favor. But this one is tough to carry off; in addition, there's the problem of the reader having to cope with the author looking into any character's mind, more or less at will. Alas for those who would fall back on this technique anyway, knowing or unknowing, the reader nowadays expects to have to cope with only a single pair of eyes through which to see the fictional world, a single pair of ears to hear with, a single set of thoughts in any one given scene. That's all that any of us have anyway, which is why the authorial omniscient unlimited POV went out of favor long ago.

Another character may look, but only the VPC can see, as others may listen but only the VPC can hear. Only the VPC can note anything—not another character in the scene. The VPC may hazard a guess at somebody's odd behavior. It's expectable that he would ask what's wrong, even. But we as readers are not allowed to peek into another character's mind and be told specifically that she's noting anything.

Sometimes you'll run across a scene where the author has cleverly shifted POV on you, only you don't even notice until later. The most usual example that comes to mind is when the VPC leaves the room but the scene inside the room goes on without him. Timing, again, dictates a bridge section of non-VPC specific text until the author gently insinuates the reader into one of the other character's heads. This is what technique is all about. The aim is to keep the reader comfortable—lulled into a sense of security that the author knows what's what, and won't pull any unwelcome surprises, or drop the reader on her head by some awkward writerly "trick." Then the reader will relax and the author can do darn near anything he wants from that point onward. It should go without saying that the author will then spin the best yarn she is capable of giving her reader. If he does, and it all works the way it should, said reader will rise up and call the author blessed.

Another POV that is a technical challenge is the *first person limited*. When this one works, it works well. When it bombs, it is a disaster. It can be hard to market if an editor has had too many close encounters with first person bombs.

The marketability of a first person narrative depends on the story being told. Its readability depends on how dexterously the writer has handled what is, really, a very taxing technique. Many of the objections to first person narrative fall into the "manly chest and lush breast" category (I crushed the maiden to my broad, manly chest—or, I gathered the warrior to my ripe, bounteous bosom—or, My softly curling blonde hair fell cascading to my tiny waist) where the author struggles with narrator descriptions that border on techniques used in poorly written porn.

Third person limited (or third person subjective) starts out in one head and stays there throughout the work. Its forced intimacy is as restricting in its own way as first person limited and, because of this, is not often used nowadays except for mystery novels. Here the constrictions work well for the type of story involved.

In *third person objective* the narrator stays coldly aloof, never penetrating below the surfaces of her characters. It is hard to think of a contemporary example of third person objective prose, as it is not only cold but also not attractive to a reader because of its lack of involvement on both sides of the page—writer and reader alike.

Essayist-omniscient is the voice of a person—the disguise the author has adopted for the purpose of telling that particular story. "Tales told around the fire" are prime examples of the essayist-omniscient tone and voice.

Here are some other sub-set POVs, with examples:

Internal, Principal Character: I was delighted to discover that I had won the record-setting lottery, so I called Stanley to come over and help me celebrate.

Internal, Secondary Character: Gwendolyn called and said she was delighted to hear that I had suddenly come into great wealth, and asked if I could come over to help her celebrate.

Internal, Composite (or Multiple): Memo from Gwendolyn to Stanley: I just heard that my lottery ticket won; will you come over and help me celebrate? Memo from Stanley to Gwendolyn: My pleasure. What time?

Internal, Detached Narrator: I could see that Gwendolyn was simply delighted to learn that she had suddenly become wealthy, and I wasn't the least bit surprised when I heard her call Stanley to come over to celebrate, and when Stanley ran all the way, the impetuous love-sick fool.

External, Full Omniscience: Gwendolyn was delighted at the news about the lottery win, and when Stanley realized how rich she was, he galloped all the way over to help her celebrate, and didn't even use a horse.

External, Limited Omniscience: Because he thought Gwendolyn would be delighted at the news about her winning ticket, Stanley hurried to help her celebrate.

External, Detached Omniscience: Stanley approached Gwendolyn in the gazebo. "Why did you come over?" she asked. "Because I think you must feel like celebrating," he replied. "I do," said Gwendolyn. "I am truly elated at the news that I am now rich beyond the wildest dreams of avarice."

If you are having trouble keeping things straight as you practice POV, you'll be able to correct this as you write if you will "label" each scene—which character it is who is "center stage," so to speak, and which one you, as author, are "playing." If you can visualize clearly enough, you'll be able to "see" the others, even as your VPC is doing, and you will realize that, as the character you have become, you really don't have any sort of clue as to what is going on in anybody else's head but your own. Also, you won't have to rely on that stale "had he but known" evasion that is all too transparent.

And that, kiddies, is why some writers are excellent actors, and vice-versa. They've had lots of practice.

We won't even approach the subject of why some writers are not excellent actors. That is not a good place to go.

Essay Six:
Plots and Non-Plots

If there is one place where beginning writers most frequently go astray it is in plot, in confusing setup with story. Let us begin to plot a short story, using good old Stanley and Gwendolyn:

> Stanley decides to go for an after-dinner walk; Gwendolyn's dumplings leave something to be desired in the digestibility department. As he is ambling down the sidewalk, he notes with absent-minded pleasure the neighborhood fireplugs which, one year in a burst of community whimsy, everyone painted to look like little people. There are soldiers, sailors—one Santa Claus—policemen, clowns, and the inevitable fireman. He is startled out of his reverie by the sight of what appears to be an ambulatory fireplug as it waddles out from behind a hedge. With a malevolent chuckle, it plants itself beside a parked car just as a police cruiser turns the corner. The cruiser stops, one of the officers jumps out, writes a traffic citation, puts it under the windshield wiper, and the officers drive on. Then the fireplug waddles away, apparently in search of another victim.
> "Aha," Stanley says to himself. "That explains a lot."
> Then Stanley returns home, vowing to himself that in future he will take another route for his after-dinner walks.

Is this a story? No, it is not. It is an Idea—the Setup. If it all ends here, then the author has backed off at just the wrong moment, and committed *fictionalis interruptus*. In order for this to be a story, Stanley must get involved with what Fate (or the author) has seen fit to send his way; and it is at this point that the possible story-lines go flying in every direction like the end of an unraveling rope. Perhaps this is an alien creature and now Stanley must repair its space ship, take it to the White House, feed it, whatever. Perhaps it is a leprechaun in drag; Stanley confronts the creature and it offers Stanley three wishes in exchange for keeping his mouth shut about what he has seen. Perhaps this is a native of Earth, a chameleon-creature heretofore undiscovered because of its uncanny ability to mimic its surroundings. This one is male; he has lost his mate when she switched forms in his absence. He is taking out his pique in making undeserving motorists get traffic tickets, and he prevails upon Stanley to help him find his mate who may be committing even more serious mischief.

Whatever happens, and it may be good, indifferent, or utterly abysmal, it is a story and not just the setup for one. Neither Stanley nor the creature—and possibly the world—will be the same after their encounter, and that's what story-telling is all about.

Constructing a novel plot is different. Most novels follow a recognizable form; we open with a character or characters with a problem, and there is a series of crises involving one or more characters as they try to solve this problem, culminating in The Big Climax where all hell breaks loose, ending in resolution. All this in 300-400 ms. pages. The single biggest hurdle in novel-writing has to be the first chapter. There are rules for constructing an opening chapter, and this is something most beginning writers do not adequately grasp.

A reader deserves to be given certain information in the first chapter of a book. He needs to be introduced to the main character(s), the one(s) primarily through whose eyes he will be observing the events chronicled in the next 400 pages or so. He needs to learn what MC's besetting problem is, the solution of which is interesting enough that the reader will be enticed into making the journey along with MC. The reader, in short, needs to be tempted and beguiled, sucked into setting aside her realities and go inhabit an author's world of lies. If the author does her job well enough, she can wind up that first chapter with enough energy that the rest of the novel will practically write itself. The author just gives it a nudge now and then to keep the level up, and can disappear and stage-manage while the characters, who have now achieved lives of their own, tell their own stories.

Many writers, particularly beginners, ignore the requirements of plot, apparently under the misapprehension that writing is this mysterious thing that occurs when the person goes into some sort of creative "trance"—communicates with the Muse—"feels" her way through some vague, half-realized story. And, alas, "creative writing" teachers just love this sort of thing; they call what results "sensitive" or sometimes "literary". Nonsense. Odds are that this "technique" hasn't produced a sensitive, let alone a literary, story so much as one that "feels" like groping one's way through a cavern filled with cobwebs thick as velvet portieres. The writer must be in charge at all times. He can't afford to give up control of his story—not even to the Muse (a/k/a LSV [q.v.] a/k/a Fred [q.v.])—because what results then becomes something quite incomprehensible to anyone but the author and those demons that haunt his mind. It is, to risk the risqué, more than a little like masturbating in public. Why masturbating? Because only the author is enjoying it. . . .

Writing by instinct, which is what this trance state is, is just one step along the way to becoming. The trick is not to stop there. We are all becoming, growing in our craft (if we're lucky and haven't short-circuited ourselves by getting stuck in the Muse-communicating mode). The quickest analogy that comes to mind is the AA one; nobody ever recovers from alcoholism. One is forever a recovering alcoholic. We are forever becoming writers—better, worse, whatever—as we keep trying to make that Muse work for us rather than the other way around.

And how, you well may ask, does one find ideas—let alone plots? Mother Miller offers the following, only slightly edited from the original, which was given her by one of the many talented people she has worked with:

"I seldom am able to dream any ideas, but I do daydream them. I sit down with pencil and paper, doodling. I think about This and I think about That, and by and by an Idea comes strolling through. We chat. If we seem to get along, down comes the paper and I've trapped it. I collect these Ideas, like stamps. Every so often, I drag them out and browse through them. And every less often, an Idea becomes a Plot. And rarely, after much labor and moaning, the Plot becomes a Story. Then the Story has to become a Submission. Much later—when the moon turns green and I catch an editor in a tolerant mood—it can become a Publication.

"The pleasant part is the daydreaming and the little chats. The rest is work."

Mother Miller couldn't have said it better herself.

Essay Seven:
Constructing a Plot in Cold Blood

Do this and trust me. I haven't let you down yet, have I?

Write the numbers 1 through 7 on a sheet of paper, or a file in your computer. Whatever feels best to you. The computer file may be best, as there you definitely will have room for a brief synopsis of your story. When you have gone through the following steps, you should have a story outline and a good start on what you really want to write.

A story starts with three elements: character, context, and conflict. These are the first three blanks in your file. Fill them in, briefly.

First you establish your main character and his resources—physical, intellectual, emotional, his possessions, training, education, and whatever else will eventually apply to the dramatic needs of the story. Never change them to fit the circumstance.

```
Beside the number 1 in your file, write
your character's name and a fact or two about
him. You can go into more details later.
```

Second, give your character *context* within which to operate. This is your setting—time, place, history, culture—a complete background which he occupies and is either at home in or not. Remember that everyone feels like somebody who got into the party on false pretenses, so a character in an uncomfortable setting is immediately interesting, and a character who is confident in his environment can be knocked off balance by story events. Context helps define character, and suggests the terms of the conflict.

All elements of character and conflict should be integrated into the fabric of the opening chapter of the novel in such a way that the reader never sees the seams. This does not mean massive info-dumps are required. Just a hint will do.

```
Beside the number 2, write a sentence
describing the context of the story.
```

Third, without conflict a story isn't a story, so a good strong believable *conflict* comes next. A story character has a dramatic need, a particular need for the purposes of the story. Readers stick around for the conflict and for suspense, not knowing what's going to happen next. For that reason, something must oppose the character's desire, and that's where conflict comes in.

In addition to a protagonist, or main character, every story also has some form of antagonist, sometimes spoken of as the villain. It's easy here. Some claim that conflict comes in three flavors—man against man, man against nature, and man against himself. Those are just the outward trappings, though; in the final analysis, it's always the character against his own problems and shortcomings, no matter what the outer conflict is that brings the inner one into focus. The antagonist enables the outer conflict, but in the end, the protagonist is battling himself.

```
Beside the number 3, write a sentence
about the story's conflict.
```

Because of this horrid thing or person or whatever now opposing him, the character must now make an attempt to *resolve* his situation. Because we can't have the story over too soon, his first attempt will fail, and because the reader loves seeing characters going through their paces like a laboratory rat, so will the second. These attempts and failures make up parts four and five of the story. After the first failed attempt to meet his need, the character will grit his teeth and show real determination, and gather his resources for a second attack at the problem. When this attack too is thwarted, he will feel that all is lost. This is known as the "black moment". Dramatic, right? You betcha. And necessary, too.

```
Beside 4, write a brief attempt and
failure sentence. Write a sentence about the
second attempt and failure beside 5.
```

Element six is *resolution.* All does indeed seem lost until the protagonist gets turned around by something called the *precipitating event,* which reactivates his resolve, and causes him to discover resources he did not know he possessed. Because you, the author, do know, you will have foreshadowed these resources at the beginning of the story, although you may not have brought them to the reader's attention as resources, and may have even disguised them as weaknesses.

Using this newfound resolve he has gathered by sheer luck and pluck, along with information he may have obtained only as a result of being defeated so soundly, the character may now push on to victory. This is the *resolution of the plot.*

If it turns out, in another story perhaps, that the protagonist is going to fail to meet his objective, the "black moment" is actually a "white moment", in which he thinks he is going to succeed, and the reader does too. Then on to his downfall.

```
Beside 6, write a sentence or two about
how the plot is resolved.
```

Finally, the seventh element is *validation,* or the resolution of the *theme.* If the plot is driven by what the character *wants,* the theme is driven by what he *needs,* and possibly what he doesn't even realize he needs. There is a question asked in some way by the story, and the validation answers it.

```
Is love/friendship stronger than fear?
What's the difference between love and need?
If someone has something special to offer the
world, what will the world do to him as
punishment?
```

The character's drive, as I see it, is almost always something entirely different. He essentially wastes time dinking around with what he wants or thinks he wants and you have to keep it interesting to the reader. It is not an easy task, but if the drive is sufficiently compelling, it can be done. When all is resolved, then all is rosy. The thunderstorms stop, the clouds part, the sun comes out, heavenly music sounds from offstage, and all is well with the world once more.

Validation occurs throughout a story, as the writer decides how to present ideas and points of view so that the reader will either feel that they are valid or invalid in this story's world view. Sometimes this is known as character growth.

> Beside 7, write a sentence about the resolution of the theme, or validation.

Now you're ready to focus and start getting your story down. To keep yourself on track, try distilling your story's plot into *one sentence* and tacking it up on the wall in front of you as you write. *This* is what your story is really about, and as long as you're writing about *this*, you won't be wandering about trying to tell some other story.

> This is a story about [FILL IN THE BLANK].

This seems to sum it up for me. You might also try writing this sentence from the point of view of the character:

> This is the story of how I had to [FILL IN THE BLANK].

You might want to keep your thematic content focused by writing another sentence about the story's theme:

> This is also a story about how [FILL IN THE BLANK].

Or whatever you decide your theme is.

Any story idea can be outlined just this simply as stated herein.

It may seem mechanical, but it works. It takes everything you need to know about your story to get started and corrals it into a manageable space and structure; from there you can go on whatever flights of fancy you please. This part is not about art; art is using your expertise in writing to affect the emotional level of the reader. Art is what happens when someone reads what you have written and is changed, however slightly, thereby. This part is about craft, and about being more in control of the writing process, thus enabling stories to happen.

This process has many parents; I first encountered it from A.J. Budrys, with his tale of Susie and the violin. It has found the light of day many times and from many people before and since, and the best thing about it is that it flat works. Try it. If you want a personal recommendation, you've got one, from me. I've done it, and done it successfully. At the very least, it's certainly worth a shot.

You may also notice that it is remarkably similar those classic journalistic questions Who, What, When, Where, Why, and How. This is no accident. They are elements that *must* be readily accessible in every sort of story, be it journalistic, a short story, or a novel.

Essay Eight:
Novel or Short Story?

What's the difference? Isn't a novel just a short story with a lot more words in it?

Well, no.

When I was writing my first novel, somebody asked me, naively I hope, about how much padding I had to add to make the tale into a novel. The fact was, I had so much sheer story to tell that I not only didn't have room for padding but also would have a task keeping the ms. down to a word count under 150,000. I fear my attempts at explanation fell on deaf ears. Only another writer who recognizes the difference in the art forms will truly understand.

Generally speaking, a short story examines one event in a character's life. A novel can, and frequently does, examine a whole constellation of events in one or more characters' lives, sometimes spanning generations.

Is it a matter of focus? Possibly. Perhaps even probably. There's one thing I've observed over the years of both teaching and writing, and that is that Novel and Short Story might as well be different languages. Some people, myself included, are natural-born Novel speakers, and others are natural-born Short Story speakers, and if we want to communicate those thoughts and ideas and notions that clutter up our heads in another form besides our native tongue, we have a learning curve ahead of us.

Yes, I have learned to speak Short Story, and the accent diminishes with each effort, but my favorite form of self-torture remains, and always will be, the Novel.

There are some forms, presentations, depictions, that simply "fit" better in short story format than trying to stretch them out to novel length. One of the best examples I can think of offhand is the wonderful short story "Flowers For Algernon" that failed miserably when it received liberal doses of that infamous padding to turn it into the novel CHARLY.

In a novel, the writer has the leisure to explore sub-plots, particularly if they impinge on the main character or characters, or affect what is going on in the body of the novel. In a short story, these sub-plots would be simply intrusive. In a novel, a writer has a greater breadth and scope. In a short story, every word, every syllable, yea, every piece of punctuation is vital and must be crafted with the greatest of care. In both, the primary purpose must be to entertain the reader and keep her enthralled. The author must remember that what doesn't help the story hurts the story, and should be chucked out without ceremony.

In a workshop setting, it sometimes becomes amusing to discover a natural novelist trying and trying to construct a short story and succeeding only in creating the first chapter of yet another novel. Been there, done that, *déjà vu* just isn't what it used to be, and that is another reason why the essay on constructing a plot in cold blood is such a godsend when nothing will do but you have to write a short story anyway.

No—as I have said before and will do so again—shortcuts. Transcribing a role-playing game session is no substitute for thinking up a plot on your own. Nor is taking one from Column A and two from Column B of other people's ideas while the creator of such an atrocity hopes that nothing is recognizable. It is, and brings no glory to anybody.

This brings us, in a curious and roundabout sort of way, to collaborations. Is it a good idea to collaborate on a novel or short story?

The answer to that question is a definite Maybe. I have collaborated on both, and generally have found the experience to be a positive one. Other people cannot say the same. Much depends on the circumstances, and also the egos involved. While I am not reluctant to admit that I am quite nicely egoized, the maintenance of my ego's health and well-being does not depend on having to have my own way all the time, and particularly when it comes to the construction of a hearty and rousing story. I've seen too many would-be collaborations that fell by the wayside when egos clashed, got in the way, and the story suffered or died. I think that this may be just one more hallmark of a professional when someone is willing to set personal considerations aside, at least temporarily, for the greater service of telling an entertaining story.

The bottom line here, as it is with many other things, is that some can and some can't, and there's no credit or blame to place if you discover that it isn't for you.

Essay Nine:
On Writing Humor

Writing humor is like hunting tiger with a popgun. In theory, the thing is possible. But oh, the consequences if you should fail. . . .

One of the reasons why it does fail, and fail so often, is that the author will forget that writing humor is a very serious proposition (like hunting tiger with a popgun). He keeps cracking jokes, trying to be funny, chortling to himself, being "clever," making every single line screamingly funny (he thinks). Showing off. And the tiger creeps ever closer.

If you read really good humorous writing with a critical eye, you will discover that, to the characters, the situation they are involved in is anything but funny, no matter how hilarious it appears to the outsider—i.e., the reader. Think about the golf game in M*A*S*H. This scene is one Mother Miller can hardly read to this day, because the tears of laughter make the page go all blurry. The author could have had Hawkeye giggle at Trapper's extremely eccentric appearance and behavior, and it would have been understandable. But it would have ruined the scene entirely. There are sections of AUNTIE MAME that have the same effect. Impossible to read aloud and difficult to read silently, as the reader has to keep putting the book down and wiping her eyes.

This is true regarding television as well. That justly famous skit wherein Lucy and Vivian are working in a candy factory and somebody speeds up the conveyer belt is vintage and very classic humor. While the audience is in stitches, neither Lucy nor Vivian are the least bit amused, you will note, even though they are stuffing chocolates in their mouths and, presumably, raising their endorphin level to an astonishing degree.

Mother Miller has written her share of humor in her time—successful humor, that is—and more than her share of unsuccessful attempts. She knows whereof she speaks. If you would write humor, you can't start any earlier than this good minute reading the masters of the craft, trying to find out how in the devil the thing is done.

Then, if you have to try your hand at humor anyway, please keep in mind that the tiger awaits, and it is always hungry....

Essay Ten:
The Write Stuff

Every writer in this world—alas, even Mother Miller—has this one biggie to overcome, and that's being in love with her own prose. Some writers never get past it, and they are the ones who finally become unreachable. One must learn to examine one's work coldly and clinically, searching for the flaws that one would really rather not find—after all, isn't one's own stuff Perfect, having come from a Genuine Perfect Person, which we all believe we are down in our heart of hearts, if we'll just be honest with ourselves? But of course.

An odd thing that writers do sometimes is assigning the same characteristic gestures to every character—particularly, for no known reason, cogitative gestures. Everyone in the story or novel will purse her lips or rub her eyebrows or crack her knuckles while thinking, and it quickly drives a reader berserk. What gets really funny is when you meet one of these writers in person and discover that he does this cogitative gesture himself!

Another pitfall to overcome is falling in love with one word, or phrase, or piece of business, and constructing a work around it. It takes a lot of skill to bring this one off, and 99% of the time, it's not successful. The seams do show.

There are two schools of thought about what constitutes the strength of a sentence. Some people think strength in writing comes from using sparkling adjectives and adverbs. Mother Miller holds the view that verbs and nouns form the framework of the sentence, like the trunk of a tree, or the iron girding of a building. Adjectives and adverbs are trimming. Or, in another context, spice. Too much spice ruins the pumpkin pie. And too many adverbs and adjectives will make for an overly ornate style.

Style is something that comes slowly and painfully. Sometimes an author can recognize her own stylistic tics and tendencies—piling on the modifiers, favorite sentence constructions, often used to excess; peculiar forms of locution (such as using "said he" instead of "he said"); over-use of weak and flabby verb forms; reiteration, stating the same thing two or more times as if not trusting the reader to understand with one reading or not trusting himself to convey the thought adequately; indulging in authorial interjection, also known as editorial comment disguised as internal dialogue; driving a favorite word into the ground, and so on. Raise your own consciousness about your stylistic excesses before someone else has a chance to.

Every writer goes through a stage of development where he indulges in a process known as Reader-Cheating. RC occurs when the author "hides" or plays coy with information—cleverly failing to identify the main character first off, making the hapless reader flail about, vainly searching for the person with whom he is going to slog along through however pages of ms., and wondering why he is bothering; neglecting to mention some important detail and leaping out from ambush and shouting "Aha!" when it is finally produced, the way a rabbit is produced out of a hat. Sometimes RC consists of a big build-up with no resolution. A shaggy-dog story is a prime example of RC. The author must constantly ask himself if there is some real (not delusory) reason the reader is not entitled to a given piece of information and, if not, why not.

A corollary to RC is where the author over-describes. Unless a reader has been living under a rock for the past several decades and doesn't, for example, know what an automobile is or how it operates, he doesn't need to have described every step of the process of inserting a key into the ignition, starting the car, and driving off explained to him—frequently, in some of the worst cases, complete with which hand is performing which operation! Over-explanation is a dreadful thing to have to read.

Lazy writers will try to flim-flam readers. They'll slip into sentimentality, trying to dazzle the reader into caring for a character they haven't taken the trouble to build as one worthy to be cared about by flag-waving, or resorting to cliche—or, in extreme cases, by simply telling the reader that he is expected to bleed for some bozo and letting it go at that. And the sensible reader abandons the story then and there.

Lazy writers will indulge in dangling participles, with never a clue as to what they've done. They will construct sentences that mean the complete opposite of what they intend, simply because they weren't paying attention. Lazy writers will commit atrocious syntax errors:

```
She put her own hand to her throat and
rubbed it to try to get some circulation into
the bloodstream.
```
    (Actually, Mother Miller likes having blood in her bloodstream, but each to her own. . . .)

And then there's:

```
I won't be able to get the blaster
phasegun due to the time for energization is
too long.
```
    (I had always wondered about what caused the delay.)

Or:

```
Commodore Jones arose from a hard cot to
stare into the eyes of a man who appeared to
have no feeling in his eyes.
```
    (Naturally it was an exercise in futility . . . .)

Mother Miller wouldn't make this up. She couldn't possibly.

A related problem occurs when the author lets the reader know, whether accidentally or on purpose, that he doesn't care a rap about his characters—that he does not respect his characters and even, in extreme cases, has contempt for them. This can come out most frequently when the author is dealing with her villain, and betrays her disapproval and lack of sympathy. And if the author feels this way, why on earth should a reader react differently? It's okay to hate despicable characters; that's what they're for. It's even better when the author can care enough about her despicable characters to be able to make the reader care also, even while he is crawling about inside his skin with disgust.

And then there's the author who simply will not get out of center stage and be content to manage the action from the wings. He insists on being right out there in the thick of things—*Look, Ma, I'm writin'!* The reader is ever conscious that there is an *author* behind all this, that the story never really happened except in this *author's* mind, that the reader is being manipulated by this *author* whose ego is more important to him than any of his characters will ever be. And again, the sensible reader does the sensible thing, choosing not to come between the author and his best beloved—himself—and sets the work aside.

Learning how to make oneself disappear, given the average writer's ego, is, to put it baldly, a bugger. But it must be done. A reader wants to become involved with, immersed in, and generally read your story, not be distracted with your waving your hand and leaping about, making certain the reader is fully conscious all the time that it's you, The Writer, who is doing this wonderful thing and it is he, merely the reader, who is relegated to the minor role of reading the glorious results. He has forgotten the big rule, that he is not the powerful one here. The reader is, for it is the reader who can decide to read or ignore the piece.

Look at it this way. A writer's job is to disappear. Your place is not onstage, nudging the reader as you show off your own cleverness or indulge in authorial interjection. You must become transparent, the window through which the story is perceived. Does the playwright upstage the actors? No? Then go and do likewise. Or don't do, actually.

Somewhere, back in the back of every writer's head, is a Little Small Voice (LSV) that will do a lot of the donkey-work for him; that will do what's necessary to build a character rather than prop up a cardboard cutout; that will whap him with the equivalent of a rolled-up newspaper if he starts getting snippy about her characters; that will gently but firmly lead him offstage to the wings where he belongs—if the author will just let it. Sometimes a writer actually fluffs off her LSV, perhaps under the misunderstanding that it is just one more voice in the myriad that fills her head with incessant chatter. You can recognize your LSV, however; it's the one who keeps searching for just the right word, who keeps jiggering with the plot to make it tighter, who re-phrases sentences over and over until they say what you intend to convey—and, on occasion, makes them sing. The other voices are, primarily, characters, saying their lines to each other. Or pieces of description, forming by molecular cohesion. But the LSV is unique and a writer worth her salt will cultivate it for the treasured resource it is.

This part of the mind, this LSV, is what Damon Knight calls Fred. Fred is the subconscious. He is astonishingly creative. However, while Fred is a wonderful research assistant, he is a very poor writer. He's the one who leaves unresolved conflicts, who scatters plot devices all over the landscape and never picks up after himself, who drops highly symbolic items throughout and never bothers to explain. The rest of the brain—the so-called rational part—is not creative. But it is tidy. If one writes from the rational portion of the brain entirely, the result is deadly, dry as dust. I submit that writing is both an art and a craft, the result of learning to tame Fred and let him supply those surprising twists and turns of plot, those glittering word choices, those powerful symbols, in a controlled environment. You, acting as your rational brain, can say to Fred, "No, this won't do. Go back and concentrate on that great idea and polish it, track it to its logical conclusion before you pop three more at me." That's how my best stuff—and Mother Miller is immodest enough to admit that some of her stuff is quite good—is made.

This may sound strange, but if you are lucky, you will eventually arrive at that most frustrating stage of development when you are incorporating your own inadequacies into your consciousness (despite Fred, who has hidden them from you for years), and your critical senses are opening to the world in general. You will discover that you don't have time to read bad writing, even your own. You will be unsure about whether your own skills are sufficient to carry you through to that golden day when you get published, and you will go into a deep depression. This is perfectly normal, depression and all, because believe it or not, this is a sign of growth. It is inward, which is what makes it so tough to endure, but it's the best kind. I have read enough garbage and claptrap to last me far more than a lifetime, perpetrated, bought and published by people who, as far as I can ascertain, have never achieved this level of growth. So how do I know all this? Because I've been there; furthermore, I go through it all over again periodically. Not many writers are even able to talk about it, for they don't recognize it for what it is—and that, perhaps, is the most depressing thing of all.

Essay Eleven:
The Eyes Have It

Lazy writers will use language in lazy ways. They will rely, for example, on characters' eyes doing strange things. This writer has collected some wonderful examples culled from various mss. through the years and the list continues to grow. So help me, these are real. My comments in parentheses follow.

>He cast his eyes about the room and they landed on a pail of water.
>
>(My all-time favorite. Naturally, this should be, "they landed in a pail of water" and people who don't use prepositions correctly have no business trying to write.)
>
>He had his eyes pressed against the screen.
>
>(Bet that smarted.)
>
>They were locked together by their eyes as they gazed at one another.
>
>(And no time off for either good or bad behavior, I'll warrant.)
>
>His eyes rolled down her figure.
>(And bounced along the floor. . . .)
>
>His eyes stared in wonderment at the spectacle before him.
>(He had left them behind inadvertently while he wandered off into the next county.)
>
>Her eyes flashed green and red sparks.
>(She was always a big hit at the office Christmas party.)

```
    His eyes wandered over the assortment of
items in the room, finally coming to rest on a
threadbare coat.
```
(...where they insinuated themselves into a pocket and started building a nest.)

```
    His eyes roamed down the corridor.
```
(Who knows what or whom they sought.)

```
    He rolled his eyes into an intense stare.
```
(The intense stare, resentful over the intrusion, rolled the eyes right back again.)

And so on, ad nauseam.

Essay Twelve:
Building Character

The character-building we're talking about here is how to build a fictional character—though many of the exercises tend to result in making us build or re-build our own as well.

Too often, the amateur writer will use characters merely as authorial puppets. They move at the writer's direction, they mouth things the author wishes to say, they change habits and characteristics at the drop of a hat. This frequently happens because the author has not understood that the characters are not the same as the author—though, simultaneously, they are. Confusing enough for you?

You must get to know your characters, inside and out. One of the best ways to do this is to do character sketches of anybody who appears more than a couple of times in your text. Do it in the notebook most writers take with them everywhere they go, so they can trap errant story ideas, descriptions, snatches of conversation, whatever. Write down everything you can think of about this character—likes and dislikes, physical description, childhood diseases, nervous tics—in short, the works. Sometime during this process the character will oblige you by coming to life and beginning to speak directly, in her own words. Then, once this has happened, the characters will, with only a little direction from the author, tell their own stories. However, to keep all this coming properly, the author must, in turn, play fair with the characters and, in so doing, with the reader. The author may not make a character do something he wouldn't do, just because the plot demands it, or because it's easier, or any of those myriad of reasons it happens. If the characters are at all worth their salt, they will promptly go on strike, creating what is known as writers' block.

Another of the talented people Mother Miller has worked with puts it this way:

> "Writing is a game. It's a great game because the author gets to make up the rules. But once he's done that, he has to play by them. When he doesn't, the reader notices and is suddenly aware that he's reading fiction. Bad. You do not want that to happen. Ever."

One of the toughest things a beginning writer has to learn, when he receives tough, accurate, caring critique from Mother Miller, is to separate the critique from the writer.

When doing a critique, I frequently get exquisitely infuriated with characters doing stupid things and say so, without inhibitions and sometimes in an entertaining manner even to the person whose characters they are. (Oh, good grief, now this idiot is sticking his head into the oven to check for a gas leak. Good. I hope he lights a match as well, blows himself to Kingdom Come and relieves this critic from having to read about such a dork. Is this how the author wants a reader to feel about her main character?) Sometimes I suggest that an author inform himself on some subject or other, so as to avoid committing the same errors again. More often, and usually by way of my Standard Lectures, I recommend that a neo-writer sharpen her grasp and command of the English language. After all, it's only the tool we possess with which we strive to tell our stories. The fact that the Standard Lectures exist is my way of making a sharp commentary on the sad state of affairs that makes such lectures necessary.

Nobody on an editorial staff is going to fix an author's microwriting errors for him; most aren't any better informed than the average neo because of the way our educational system has gone to hell in a handbasket since, roughly, the 60's. We have to do it ourselves and acquire such a firm knowledge of our craft that no little second-year lit. major working part-time as an editorial assistant would dare monkey with the structure of our prose and if the assistant does dare, be able to intimidate and refute him and cite chapter and verse as to why and how. (Works wonders every time; I know whereof I speak.)

I have yet to attack a writer, however, and only those who mistake their words for themselves have ever perceived my critiques as such. If someone takes an honest critique personally, that neo has learned a valuable lesson thereby—that writing is not the career for him.

Following you will find an amazingly comprehensive form for Character Building. Do this a few times, just for the drill. By the time you get through with this, you will know that character better than her own mother could or perhaps would want to. Later, you will be able to take a shortcut or two but right at first, you need the practice.

CHARACTER BUILDER

```
Story (circle one):   Novel Short Story
Date story starts:
Name of Character:
Nickname(s):
Alias, if any:
```

This outline is to indicate the character's status at the start of the tale. The character's growth evolves from this point.

Please note that the reader doesn't have to have all this information, but the writer should know it.

PHYSICAL CHARACTERISTICS:

```
Age:
Sex:
Birthdate:
Birthplace:
Height:
Weight:
Color of hair:
Color of eyes:
Nationality:
Race:
```

Habitual expression in repose or when no one is looking:

Habitual posture:

Style of dress:

Manner of speech:

Way of
    gesturing:
    moving:
    walking:

Does character have any physical scars, birthmarks, handicaps, or extraordinary features? Describe.

Does character have any health problems? Describe.

Briefly describe character's overall appearance.

HISTORY/BACKGROUND:

Education
Amount:
    Kind of schools:
    Marks:
    Favorite subjects:
    Poorest subjects:
    Aptitudes:

Work experience or skills
    Occupation:
    How long on current job:
    Schedule:
    Income:
    Work conditions:
    Union or non-union:
    Character's suitability for work:

What incident of childhood affected character the most?

    Friends
        Best:
        Male:
        Female:

    Enemies or minor antagonists, and why:

    Family
        Are parents living?
        Mother:
        Father:
        History of parents
          (occupations, married, divorced, etc.)
        Siblings:
        Brothers:
        Sisters:
        Half-brothers:
        Half-sisters:
        Step-brothers:
        Step-sisters:

    Character's marital status
    To whom is/has character been married?
        Why did character marry spouse?
        If separated, why?
        Does character have any children?
            Sons:
            Daughters:
            Step-sons:
            Step-daughters:

    Describe character's home.
    Does character share residence with anyone?
        Who and why?

    Does character have any pets?
        How many?
        What kind?

What are pets' names?

Hobbies:

Kinds of music, art, reading material, sports preferred:

Who has had greatest influence on character:

What does character most regret?

What opportunities did character miss?

What class is character in?
   Lower
   Middle
   Upper
What is character's place in community? Leader? Non-leader?

What are character's political affiliations?

PERSONALITY/CHARACTER TRAITS:

What is character's overwhelming passion?

Describe character's personal and general attitudes toward
   Family:
   Marriage:
   Money:
   Religion:
   Sex:
   Politics:

Ambitions, personal goals:

Favorite color(s):

Favorite pastime(s):

What does character hate most
    Food:
    Color:
    Activity:
    Traits in others:

List character's proudest achievements:

What has character done for which he/she is most ashamed?

Is character basically introverted or extroverted?

What kind of sense of humor does character have?

Describe character's favorite fantasy.

How do others see character?

How do others react to character?

Describe what character tries hardest to avoid
    In general:
    Simple daily routines:
    Chief taboos:
    Chief fears:

Is character self-centered, and if so, how?

What kind of person would character like to be?

Describe how far away character is from this ideal
    Subjectively:
    In the opinion of others:

How does character see future?

What is character's philosophy of life?

What makes life worthwhile for character?

What is worth dying for?

What are character's strong points?

What are character's weak points?

Does character promise to do things and then forget?

When a person is telling an incident or story, does character always try to outdo with one of his/her own?

Does character have clique of friends from which he/she excludes others?

Does character tell friends what is wrong with them?

Does character like to be center of attention all the time?

Does character make loans to friends?
    Does character let everyone know about it?
    Some people but not others?
    No one?

Can character keep a secret?

Does character call on people to perform trivial tasks for him/her?

Would character drop everything if a friend needed help?

Is it easy for character to find good things about others?

Is character someone who drops in and then forgets to "pick him/herself up" again?

What abilities does character have?
    Foreign languages, talents, etc.

What is character's general intelligence level?

Describe character's attitudes and practices concerning chemical substances
    Caffeine:
    Tobacco:
    Marijuana/recreational drugs:
    Alcohol:

GENERAL DESCRIPTION:

Describe character in one sentence.

If working on a novel, write a short biography if this is a main character.

Essay Thirteen:
Building Bad Character; Villains and Other Despicable Beans

When you start to construct a villain, remember that nobody—not even Hitler, Stalin, Messalina, Nero, you name it—ever woke up in the morning saying to himself, "Oh, goody, another bright and shining day when I can go out and do some evil!" If you let your Bad Guy rub her hands and gloat over what a s**t (or *hi*, take your pick) she's being, that's rubber-stamp rejection time from editors or, say the editor was asleep and this kind of villain did see print, *thpft*-rejection time from readers. It's also a copout—taking the easy way. Label the guy bad and then you don't have to mess with building his character. Writing isn't supposed to be easy, or everybody would be doing it. Trust me, building a really swell, complicated villain is bags of fun, and the result is much more enjoyable to read about.

But how to go about it?

In each of us flawed human beans, no matter how good or exemplary we think ourselves (Mother Miller is certainly a genuine Beautiful Bean and All-Round Perfect Person—aren't you?), there exists the capacity for quite breathtaking viciousness, cruelty, larceny, perversity, murder—in short, all those great and wonderful things that make for juicy villainy. Loathsome as it might be, it is necessary to our development as complete humans for us to accept these less-than-lovely parts of ourselves, to integrate them, and, by so doing, to put them under our conscious control.

Many people are understandably loath to do this. They simply don't want to know what lies beneath the surface. Others have a suspicion, but don't want to talk about it.

The writer has to go one step further—to develop the knack of drawing upon this fine cesspool in order to depict her characters in a convincing manner. It is not enough for you, as author, to tell the reader that your villain is a sociopath who ought to be kept chained to a wall. You must let the reader into this person's mind, let the reader experience his thoughts, feelings and emotions—convince the reader to bleed when he gets cut—and try to make your audience understand him, even when they are hating everything he stands for. And where do you get all this? From that very same cesspool that underlies your normally sweet and charming self.

And people wonder why writers are sometimes just a tad weird.

Essay Fourteen: Criticism and Workshops

Criticism isn't fun, goodness knows. But it's necessary. That's why there are workshops to help us spot our errors, and help us overcome them. Workshops are better than friends, neighbors, or your mother because, if you're in the right kind of group, you can count on your workshoppers not to be kind. You won't learn a thing if you are rewarded for mediocrity; you'll just keep on turning out mediocre work.

Avoid workshops where everybody reads her work aloud. You are dealing with a visual art form, not an oral one. The best and most effective technique yet developed for operating a writers' workshop is one where everyone gets a copy of a story at one session and is expected to read and mark it up for critique at the next; this time-consuming process usually takes two readings and occasionally three. Do not read your work aloud except at home when you are checking for awkward prose. Tape recorders were made for this kind of exercise. The clunky places—the ones that trip your tongue and fall harshly on the ear and, by extension, the eye—will stand out vividly when you play it back. Or you could read it to the cat. Cats love to be read to; they think it is excruciatingly funny. Furthermore, if the cat walks out or falls asleep at the most exciting part, you know you've got more work to do.

During the critique, the person whose work is under scrutiny must sit in stoic silence while the other workshop members, in turn and one at a time, deliver their critiques, starting in a clockwise direction from that person. Each session must have a leader to moderate and keep members from talking out of turn. It avoids arguments if the leaders are chosen in a strict alphabetical order. Set a five minute time limit and have the leader keep track of the time; if you can't deliver an adequate critique in that time, you aren't doing it right. In the case of a longer work, say, a complete novel, expand the time limit. Don't repeat another's critique; either say "I agree with Joe about the broken pop-gun" or, if you have nothing at all to say that hasn't already been said, just say "Pass." As consolation for having to time everyone, the leader gets to go last and, often, can formulate a much better critique from listening to what everyone else has to say. Once everyone has had his turn, then the leader calls for seconds. Then and only then, does the author get to speak. This is often followed, in the case of a really provocative work, by a general discussion.

The object of a writers' workshop is not to demolish another writer's work, nor to show off one's own cleverness with one-liners, nor to get laughs at another's expense—though all of these elements enter into the process of critique at one time or another. The object of a workshop is for writers to help their fellow writers develop to their best potential and, in the process, learn more about the craft as they do so. Remember, it is possible to jeer any work to death. Any work whatsoever.

When a workshop is working dynamically, a bonding forms among its members that is a kind of kinship. You can tell whether yours is working right if this bonding occurs.

You are not allowed to criticize the genre. If stories about werewolves or fairies or South Seas romances give you the hives, then scratch all you like—but do it on your own time. You must develop enough professionalism to be able to handle each story on its own merits, regardless of the subject matter.

This seems as good a place as any to mention online workshops, this being the computer age and all. It's been a while since I ran an online workshop, and I am immodest enough to state that mine was a darned good one. There are plenty of other workshops out there, and some are also good. Others are not. Some are, like mine, run with an iron hand to eliminate, or nearly eliminate, the flaming and backbiting and other destructive elements that, too often, creep in to the critique process. The facelessness of an online workshop has both its good and its bad sides. You don't have to watch somebody's face when he cuts your brainchild to ribbons, or, conversely, you don't have to hide your own great glee when one of your compatriots praises what you slaved over. Sometimes, alas, this anonymity works to everyone's disadvantage. There are those who thrive on it so they can deliver as much hurt and outright harm to others as they can manage, and not suffer any sort of retribution. Be warned.

Another online pitfall is the outfit that promises to "fix" your story so it is a sure-fire sale. This doesn't really fall under the workshop category, but it seems reasonable to suppose that the unscrupulous will have no hesitation in trolling online workshops in hopes of attracting the unwary, the eager, and the doomed—particularly if they get their hands on the poor beginner.

Online or face-to-face, your requirements will be the same. If you find a good workshop and it gives you good feedback and tips for improvement, stick with it. If you come away from each session feeling bad, or drained, or cut down, or otherwise slathered with negativity, run, do not walk, to the nearest exit. You deserve better.

The Golden Rule applies here. If you want to receive good critique, you'd better learn to give good critique. Keep in mind that the story you are doing the critique on is not your story. You may offer suggestions for the author to consider in fixing the rough spots, but you are not allowed to re-write the story for him. If someone tries to do so anyway (You ought to put in dwarves and elves and let them fight green-furred bats), the author is at full liberty to tell that person if he thinks it's such a wonderful idea, by all means write it down and submit it to the workshop.

Try to find at least one thing good to say. There is a difference between critique and criticism. Critique is positive in nature, aimed at helping the author improve the work. Criticism is, by and large, negative, and is much easier to do.

Make an effort to learn the tools of your craft in addition to the tools of critique. Chances are you have blank spots in your education; most of us do. If you are shaky on grammar, punctuation, spelling, proper use of homonyms and homophones, etc., work on these shortcomings. There are plenty of books available. Learn what microwriting is—the way in which the language is handled—and to recognize sloppy microwriting when you see it. Learn to recognize clunky prose. Learn the difference in those wretched verbs sit/set, lie/lay, and the proper use of the apostrophe. Learn to analyze the motivations and internal logic—or lack of it—in a story and how motivation differs from authorial manipulation. Learn to spot frigidity in writing (that is, empty prose without any real depth or meaning), how to avoid overly ornate, Latinate language (that is, fancy ten-dollar words derived from Latin rather than snappy single-syllable Anglo-Saxon derivatives) in inappropriate situations, how to maintain tension in action scenes, to shift from the lazy writer's tendency toward "tell-me" into the immediacy of "show-me." Learn what a story is, as opposed to a vignette or an anecdote. Read, read, read with an eye toward what makes a story work for you, and what makes a story fall flat. Expect to have reading for pleasure spoiled forever as you begin unconsciously analyzing everything you read—and expect also to have the rare and exquisite joy of encountering a writer whose work is so superior that you lose yourself and don't even realize it until you've finished the story.

Most readers approach a story willing to be beguiled, and the writer really has to try to bounce them out of the dream. Few workshop members and no editors are that forgiving.

Strive to separate the writer from the work; just because he put together a ms. with some bad writing and atrocious errors in it, that doesn't mean he is a bad and/or atrocious person for having done it. (He may not have any writing talent, but that's another matter altogether.) Ego-stroking isn't the purpose of workshopping. But positive support is. When something strikes you as exceptionally good, say so. That helps make up for the times when you have to trounce somebody's ego-child.

The urge to write is endemic among humans in general; unfortunately, too many people don't realize that writing fiction is as artificial an art form as is dancing ballet or singing opera. The professionals make it look easy when there is nothing easy about it. There is another urge at work here as well, and that involves keeping what one has written stashed away and out of the reach of potentially accurate criticism—"accurate" being the key word here.

One trick on accepting criticism, is to note whether it tickles that spot in the region of your solar plexus, and makes another nagging little voice go off, the one that says, "Neener neener neener, thought you could get away with that one, didn't you" and other rude comments. If it does, better listen. That's the Watcher Within, and it's almost never wrong. Maybe it's the LSV in the writer's head, throwing her voice. Other things, such as factual references, grammar, spelling, etc., are simply part of writerly craft and technique, and as such, aren't so tied in with ego. Also, if you get several people commenting about the same thing bothering them, whatever the reason and even if it doesn't make the ticklish spot go off, you'd better take a long, hard look anyway because something is definitely wrong.

If it's worth its salt, your workshop is going to be the toughest on you as a writer; it'll be tougher than any editor on the scene today. Paradoxically, the easiest to please is the reader who comes to your story wanting to be beguiled; the writer has to work at disengaging this person, but it can be done. Alas, part of the price you pay for learning the art of critique is that never again do you approach a work (except consciously) in Average-Reader Mode. It's a luxury you simply can't afford. Once in a while you'll run up against some criticism that rearranges the fillings in your teeth. There's a time and a place for this kind of super-harsh criticism—primarily when an otherwise good writer puts out a story that's sheer crap. At one time or another every one of us has been guilty of it, and when we are, we need to be yanked up by the scruff of the neck, shaken, and told, "Don't do this!"

But if it's done just to show off and otherwise demonstrate someone's (self-perceived) superiority, then slough it off and find somebody to critique your stuff who doesn't have so much ego involved. A good question to ask one's self at times like that—what does this person have to gain by saying these things? If it's nothing whatsoever, as in the case of a really good workshop, then you'd better listen. If it's jealousy or some other less-than-noble impulse on the part of the other person, then blank it out. The trick lies in knowing which kind you're dealing with.

However, workshoppers aren't the most vicious folk you'll run into vis-a-vis criticism. Critics are—the kind who write columns and who dearly love to demolish someone who has had the temerity to get published. If a writer is so fragile he can't take some fairly severe scruff-shaking in a positive workshopping environment, he will never survive the Real World out there where folks lurk who want to demolish him and will, if necessary, take any old unfair way to do it. Better to learn this early and get out while there's still time, and start a new and respectable career selling aluminum siding. Writers have to be tough while still being sensitive, and that's only one reason why it's such a rotten way to make a living and those who can be discouraged from attempting it, should be.

This admonition springs from a deep understanding of how wretched a writer's life really is. When he isn't writing, naturally he is miserable. But when he is writing, he is equally miserable, because the product falls so far short of what he wanted it to be. It's a lose-lose situation, which explains why many of us ink-stained wretches become fond of altered states of consciousness.

Remember that writing is damnably hard work. But then, nobody ever promised that it would be easy.

Recommended Books

Somewhere along the line—if you haven't begun this already—you are going to acquire a library of reference books. Many of them will be on every subject under the sun, including those in which you had only a brief and passing interest, but the backbone of your reference library must be books on your own craft. In addition to the one you are currently holding in your hand—and a wise choice it is, too—you'll want to get these standard volumes:

- William Strunk, Jr. & E.B. White—*The Elements of Style*
- John Gardner—*The Art of Writing*
- *The Chicago Manual of Style*
- H. W. Fowler—*Modern English Usage**
- William Sloan—*The Craft of Writing*
- Percy Lubbock—*The Craft of Fiction*
- William Knott—*The Craft of Fiction***
- The biggest, best dictionary you can afford
- And the other books as needed for special areas. Thousands of them.

*Get an old edition of this work. The most recent edition has been botched by hands other than Fowler's.
**Different book, different author, same title.

Essay Fifteen:
You Could Always Look It Up

There's an old, honored and cherished axiom that you should write what you know. Lots of people don't even think about this, and take it to mean that you should write *only* what you, yourself, have personally experienced. This is why most first novels are autobiographical. And most of them are virtually unreadable to boot.

What this saying really means is that you should know what you write. Furthermore, you should know it before you even sit down at the keyboard. This means the Dreaded R-Word. Research. If, say, you have decided to write a book whose plot turns on the mating habits of gerbils during some Ice Age or other, you have quite a task ahead of you. You must learn not only the mating habits of present-day gerbils, but also pick your Ice Age and learn about the climatic, geographic, and archeological conditions that would have influenced these habits back then. You must learn much more about Ice Ages and gerbils than you ever thought it possible to know, and then you must leave most of this out of the story.

Why? Because it won't be pertinent. What it will do, which is the important point, is build a solid foundation for you, the writer, so that when you do mention gerbils in the context of your overall story, the reader isn't going to be inclined to question your authority. If you try to fake it, you'll get caught every single time, no matter how delightfully vague you get, or how fancy a dance you can do around your missing data, hoping that nobody will notice. Here's another of the many True Things contained in this book: There's always somebody out there who will know more about a given subject, even the mating habits of gerbils during an Ice Age, than you ever will, no matter how much research you have done. And you think you can slide past it?

How do you know when you have done enough research? I've been in this boat, having researched the Mycenaean Age for three heavy-duty historical novels set pre-, during, and post-Trojan War. And you know what? I can't tell you when enough is enough. All I can do is tell you that if you are lucky, you will know. Speaking personally, I reached a point where I felt oddly out of place in the 20th Century. While that may have been overdoing it a bit, it worked for me. And it gave me a solid background and foundation for the tales I wanted to spin. More than one reader has told me it felt like being there. Higher praise and all that.

One of the pitfalls is the temptation to blab everything you learned, whether about the shape and configuration of shoulder-brooches in Mycenaean times or chilly gerbils in a romantic mood, regardless of how hard or how awkwardly you have to hammer in the information. In critique parlance, this is called, "I've Suffered For My Craft (and now you're damn well going to suffer, too)" and is a real turnoff not to mention a bore and a chore to read through.

Stick the leftovers in a file or, more likely, back into some corner of your mind where you put the other seldom-used but interesting facts you are always accumulating against the chance you might need them some day. It's one more of the sigh-producing aspects of this wretched life you've chosen, and will make you a whiz at the right kind of Trivia game.

Do not rely on secondary or tertiary sources! If you read a novel by Joe Whoever who happens to have mentioned Ice Age gerbils, this is no indication that Joe even read much on the subject, let alone seriously researched it. Joe may have gotten it all wrong. As per the title of this essay, if you're in the least doubt about a given detail, not only *could* you look it up, you must do so.

Let's say it all in unison: There are no short-cuts. Not if you want to be taken seriously.

Aren't you lucky that you have Mother Miller to explain this to you?

Essay Sixteen:
Bogeys, Pet Peeves, and Other Stuff

Cohort

There are some misuses of the language that will send the calmest, most mellow person into a frenzy. One of these for Mother Miller is the misuse of "cohort" to mean minion, accomplice, or companion. A cohort is a tenth of a Roman Legion, or about 600 men, and that's one hell of a lot of minions.

Cohort is a perfectly good word, and useful as well as long as the writer confines himself to using it when designating members too numerous to be counted of some sort of united group, and especially when implying some sort of struggle or contest.

Nearly the Right Word

People who carelessly grab the first word that sort of sounds like what the writer might have intended will raise blood pressure to alarming heights in those readers who recognize the difference. Actual examples: denigrated, for degenerated. Inclining, for inkling. Then instead of than. Loose instead of lose. Mother Miller would give more examples, but her blood pressure suddenly shot up much too high and she must go lie down for a while. (See the comments on "for a while" in the Standard Lectures section.)

Both writer and editor are at fault here—the writer for being so lazy and careless in the first place, and the editor for not having the wit and/or education to recognize the error.

Alright

This isn't a legitimate word. It is another one of those lazy constructions that is trying to worm its way into the language where it can chew away the underpinnings. Use it only when you are depicting a piece of illiterate writing perpetrated by an undereducated rustic. When I encounter it in a ms., I have been known to excise the abomination from the paper entirely. I really, really, do not like this at all. See further comments in the section on Standard Lectures.

Alot

This is the horrid twin to "alright" and is just as illiterate. To my intense dismay, I have learned that some teachers, ignorant themselves, are even teaching this abomination to their hapless students. We may be doomed. I also have a few extra words to say on this one in the Standard Lectures.

Decimate

This word comes to us through the Latin, from the stem that also gives us decimal, referring to ten. A few centuries ago, if you happened to be a soldier in a Roman army and the order to decimate was given, you numbered off and if you were Number Ten, you were promptly marched off and executed. This disciplinary action did wonders for the troops' morale. Today, we don't decimate our armies but the application of the word in place of "devastate" (see NTRW, above) is the mark of the under-educated. A tenth is still a tenth. If an enemy is decimated (not devastated), 90% of him remains, ready, willing, and probably entirely able to whack your ears off.

Split Infinitives

The split infinitive is a pedantic bogey carried over from the Latinate prescriptions of the 19th century. There is no such thing as a split infinitive in Latin, because each Latin infinitive is a single word. For example, "to hold" in Latin is "tenere." Thus, an expression such as "to fully hold the water" was literally impossible in Latin. Therefore, the pedants reasoned that both elements of an English infinitive should be considered as fused into one, unsplittable and sacrosanct. Only that's not the way English works.

There are no hard and fast rules. The consensus is that split infinitives should be unsplit when too many adverbial elements intrude and cause perplexity by their very number. If it sounds right to your ear and aids in clarity, then split the damned thing and go on. Proceed with caution, but not in fear.

Verisimilitude

Remember what Mark Twain said about re-creating reality. Mother Miller is paraphrasing, but it goes something along these lines: Fiction must follow certain rules in order to achieve verisimilitude. Real life, not being required to follow any rules whatsoever, is, as a consequence, completely unbelievable.

In other words, if you're drawing on personal experience, you may have to monkey with your facts in order to make them into a good story. Be prepared.

Literally

Really? Literally means, well, literally—"in a literal manner", or, as it is written. I'm not the first to complain. This gripe has been going on for well over a hundred years over the incoherency of using "literally" as meaning "virtually" or "figuratively." The misuse doesn't stem from a change in the meaning of the word, but from an unfortunate tendency to use it as a general intensive. This is literally destroying the meaning and the impact of the word.

Unique

Unique means "the only one of its kind" or "without an equal or equivalent; unparalleled." It does not mean "different" or "unusual", and can take precious few modifiers. I mean, how "almost unique" can "something that stands alone" be? To use it carelessly is illegal, immoral, and, for all I know, fattening. Stop doing it now.

Essay Seventeen:
Mother Miller's Standard Lectures
(all-too-frequently used in ms. criticism)

Why There Is No Standard Lecture 1

This, if it exists, is Standard Lecture One, and here's how it goes. Writing is not a natural act.

People will inevitably come back at Mother Miller with the claim that it is so, too. It's easy. They learned how to do it in grade school! Well, there's writing, and then there's writing. One is the physical act of forming words and letters. The other, the one we're talking about here is taking those words and actually telling a coherent story with them.

Big difference.

Writing can't be a natural act any more than singing opera or dancing ballet is. Anybody can hum along to a tune or even dazzle himself in the shower, but can everybody do justice to "La Boheme"? Anybody can jiggle more or less in time to the music, but are you any challenge to Baryshnikov? Or even John Travolta?

Do you have any idea how many failed ballet dancers and failed opera singers there are out there? Let's not even start with other forms of dancing or singing. And these people, the ones who didn't make it, studied and worked like rats to learn their art and their craft.

So what makes people think they can "write" without studying the art and the craft of it? Why do they think they can tell stories without having a clue about story structure, or how to compose a good, clear sentence, or where to put the question marks and why it is almost never a good idea to start a sentence with a comma? Or how, for that matter, the language works? The English language is the only tool we have with which to try to tell the stories that keep floating around in our brains, and if we don't bother to learn it, it is precisely analogous to a carpenter deciding to build a house out of Kleenex because a wood product is a wood product and also he doesn't know how to use other forms of wood.

Slush piles are filled with manuscripts from people who think that they don't have to bother with all these boring details such as plot or characterization, or even good grammar let alone punctuation or any of the other myriad details that make up the craft of the art, the art of the craft. Reading slush like this puts editors in very bad, grumpy frames of mind and makes it just that much tougher on the rest of us. It isn't always easy to correct bad habits, to learn what should have been instilled regarding the mechanics of the language when people were in grade school, but it is necessary. If you didn't get it then, you have to acquire it now, and that's a fact.

Standard Lecture 10: Okay. Okay, in anything but a contemporary, modern story, is definitely not okay in the least degree when writing in another time and place! This is such a jarring anachronism that it doesn't merely drop the reader out of the milieu in which the author is trying to place her, it hurls her out and slams the door shut. Never use "okay" in a medieval fantasy.

Standard Lecture 12: Unnecessary mystification. Author is dangling bits of near-information in front of the reader. It reacts on him exactly like standing around feeling foolish while someone gossips with a third party about matters he knows nothing about—or, as far as he knows, isn't likely to learn. And it is just as rude. Instead of prodding the reader into wanting to know more, it turns him off in a hurry. Why? Because he is expected to leap about like some demented lap-dog, straining after the tidbit kept tantalizingly out of reach. So the sensible reader, at this point, closes the book or story and goes away.

Standard Lecture 15: Less and fewer stand in exactly the same relationship as much and many. A person cannot have less friends any more than he can have much friends. And these people cannot be fewer friendly any more than they can be many friendly. Fewer (and many) refer to number; less (and much) refer to value, degree, or amount—as in, "Gwendolyn had fewer (or a lesser number of) new dresses since she married Stanley, and each dress cost less (or fewer dollars) than she had been accustomed to spending on her wardrobe."

Standard Lecture 16: Author mistakes "nauseous" (the state or condition of being sickening) for "nauseated" (the state or condition of being sick). In other words, you may be nauseous all you like, but you are making me ill.

Standard Lecture 17: This is flabby, passive tell-me when it should be show-me. Show-me is lively and interesting. It is hard to write, because the author has to work at getting inside people's heads, making sure various details are correct, etc. Tell-me is much easier. The author can dispose of enormous matters in a few words. It is also deadly and dull. Which would you rather read—the breathless accounting of the earthquake and the struggles the hero and heroine had to stay alive both during the quake and the confusion thereafter, or a brusque statement that the earthquake killed thousands and the hero and heroine survived? If you pick the second option, maybe fiction writing isn't for you.

Standard Lecture 18: "Alright" is not correct usage; it is substandard. The blend doesn't provide a single nuance of meaning as the blends of altogether/all together, almost/all most, already/all ready, etc., accomplish, forming as they do, adverbs. "Alright" means, simply, "all right". And it is, simply, illiterate. Use it only if you are also willing to use "alwrong," "alwet," "alclear," "alround," "AlSaints' Day," "alstar," "altold," and other barbarisms.

Standard Lecture 20: This is just one more in a long string of Amazing Coincidences. Plot requires more than Amazing Coincidences.

This sort of thing just doesn't happen, even in real life. Please find another way to do this besides having the Amazing Coincidence suddenly appear and solve it all for your characters.

Standard Lecture 24: There is no such word as "alot." "A lot" is two words. Never use "alot" except when you are showing the reader something an uneducated person has written. It is such an illiterate barbarism it notifies the reader at once that this is a person who does not know or care for the English language.

Standard Lecture 26: Filtration. For each story there is the proper tone and amount of involvement desired between reader and what is happening on the page. This is known as "distance." Beginning writers frequently put too much distance between the reader and the story with off-putting techniques such as filtering the experiences through a character's sensibilities (Stanley felt the warmth of the fire as it blazed on the seat of his pants just out of his line of sight). Finding the right distance—and sticking with it, not drawing back at just the wrong moment—is something each author must learn for himself, as it can't be taught. It can only be sensed by readers when it is right—or, more frequently, when it is wrong and disturbing.

Standard Lecture 27: Older man/woman? Older than what? Dirt? The hills? This is a flabby, imprecise construction, an unresolved comparison, that should be eradicated from every educated person's vocabulary. If he looks like a man in his sixties, say so. If she is a woman in her thirties among a group of teenagers, say so. Same thing goes for "younger" in this context.

Standard Lecture 28: Inappropriate use of passive voice. An astonishing number of times, an author will attempt to distance himself from a subject that makes him personally uncomfortable by slipping into passive voice. There is nothing wrong with passive voice per se; it has its proper use when the action is more important than the actors (war was declared), or the actors are unknown (the school was vandalized). But for most prose use and particularly in sex or action scenes, even if the author is uneasy having to deal with the subject, passive voice is just too tired to carry the burden.

Standard Lecture 29: "Mused" is the wrong word. It is also a Said-Bookism, which simply compounds the error. It is wrong because the situation does not allow it to be right. Muse, v. i., comes from the Latin mussare, meaning to murmur, mutter, be in uncertainty. The modern meaning is to ponder; to meditate; to think closely; to study in silence; to be absent in mind; to be deeply occupied in study or contemplation. None of these conditions exist.

Standard Lecture 32: More importantly is as illiterate a construction as morely important. It is either important, importantly, or more important—but not some mish-mash of these elements.

Standard Lecture 33: Different than. The preposition "than" implies a comparison with some criterion or datum. This building may be higher than that one in the next block, one car may be better than another; it specifies a direction between two quantities. The adjective "different" implies a divergence or departure between two items without specifying direction. Thus, this rose is different from that rose; one is not the same as the other in some way, which may be either higher or lower, better or worse, etc. To say this rose is different than that rose is to commit an error in logic because one is comparing and contrasting in the same sentence. As final proof, one would never say "This rose differs than that rose."

Standard Lecture 34: Author consistently uses three-dot ellipses at ends of sentences. An ellipsis within a sentence is three spaced dots. An ellipsis at the end of a sentence is four spaced dots. The fourth dot takes the place of the missing period. If a publisher's style dictates three-dot ellipses, then so be it; in the meantime, THE CHICAGO MANUAL OF STYLE says four dots.

Standard Lecture 35: Author uses ellipses where em-dashes are called for. Ellipses conventionally signal a trail-off, where the em-dash indicates a broken thought or speech, an interruption whether by the speaker or thinker, or someone else.

Standard Lecture 36: A long speech by a single character, broken into paragraphs, is terribly distracting to the reader. A new paragraph conventionally signals a new speaker. When a speech is broken into paragraphs, as here, the only signal that the speaker has not changed is a negative one—the lack of a closing quote mark at the end of a preceding paragraph—and is all too easily overlooked by the reader, who gets dreadfully confused. Experienced writers, who do not wish to confuse their readers, find ways to avoid doing this.

Standard Lecture 37: Incorrect homophone. Because English has borrowed words from every other language on Earth, inevitably there are sound-alikes with entirely different meanings in the lexicon. Perhaps in a perfect world, homophones will be abolished. But until then, this author must learn the difference between to and too; a bear heel and a bare heal; surf and serf; wench and winch; since and sense; peek, peak and pique; and many, many more.

Standard Lecture 38: Nearly The Right Word. NTRW is a disease afflicting those who are too lazy or otherwise unwilling to make friends with their dictionaries. Please look up this word at once, make friends with it, and you will never again use it in this fashion.

Standard Lecture 39: For awhile. "Awhile" is an adverb, meaning, "for a while; for a short time." Therefore, to write "for awhile" is to write "for for a while."

Standard Lecture 42: The verb "to dive" is a regular (weak), intransitive verb (does not take a direct object), not an irregular (strong) verb. It forms its principal parts from adding -ed, -d, or -t to the infinitive. Thus, "dive" becomes "dive, dived, dived." Were it not so, the declension would be "dive, dove, divven." Though it is rapidly gaining ground in spoken English, "dove" as past tense of "dive" is sub-standard form in prose, not approved among the educated.

Standard Lecture 44: Info dump, a/k/a expository lump. Action stops dead in the water, while author or agent delivers lecture. Break up the lump of indigestible matter and scatter it throughout the ms., at appropriate spots. If all the information doesn't get integrated, and integrated naturally so the seams don't show, then that's a good sign it wasn't necessary to the story. And most of it isn't, too. It hardly ever is.

Standard Lecture 45: Info dump residing between parentheses. Parentheses contain parenthetical material—a side thought, unrelated to the material in the sentence—and many if not most readers simply skip over anything in parentheses without reading it. For this reason, writers are well advised to avoid parentheses at all costs.

Standard Lecture 46: "As You Know Bob." The most pernicious form of Info Dump in which the characters tell each other things they already know, for the sake of getting the reader up to speed. Sometimes called maid-and-butler dialogue.

Standard Lecture 48: Hopefully. Hopefully means, literally, full of hope. Full of hope, the weather will be clear for the picnic tomorrow. Please do not add to the general disintegration of the English language by continuing to misuse the word to mean other than what it is.

Standard Lecture 49: Weasel-word. There are many weasel-words. Seemed, some kind of, almost, nearly, practically, well nigh, rather, and that all-time evergreen favorite, slightly. Be chary with your use of these tentative qualifiers and use them only when nothing else will do—as, when your characters are lost in a pea-soup fog and nothing can be clearly ascertained.

Standard Lecture 51: Lost antecedent. The author may know perfectly well what or to whom this refers, but the reader, not being privy to the strange goings-on in the author's head, is not.

Standard Lecture 53: English has taken a few words from other languages—notably French—and retained the differences in spelling for the genders. Blond=male; blonde=female. Likewise, brunette=female (you have to get around a dark-haired male's description another way); fiance=male, fiancee=female, and so on.

Standard Lecture 54: Breaking Wind. Indulging in a private, inside joke or inappropriate humor in front of strangers. An author who does this fails to realize that certain assumptions or jokes are not shared by the world at large. In fact, the world at large will look upon such a writer as if he had just committed a gross breach of decorum in public.

Standard Lecture 55: This is a Card Trick in the Dark, or, an authorial trick to no visible purpose. When performing Card Tricks in the Dark, the author contrives an elaborate plot to arrive at a) the punch line of a joke no one else will get (closely related to Breaking Wind), or, b) some bit of historical trivia. If the point of the story is that an obscure kid is going to grow up to be Joseph of Arimathea or Hitler's long-lost son, there should be sufficient internal evidence for the reader to figure this out on her own without the author resorting to trickery.

Standard Lecture 56: Stylistic tic, hanging action phrases onto vocal tags. ("Hello, Gwendolyn," Stanley said, walking the poodle and brushing his hair.) Don't do this. It becomes distracting, and frequently produces silly results. It also intimates concurrent actions when very probably none exist.

Standard Lecture 57: Dangling modifier. Dangling modifiers are verbal phrases (participial, gerund, infinitive) or elliptical clauses which do not refer clearly and logically to the appropriate word in the sentence and which, therefore, attach themselves to another—frequently with ludicrous results.
Dangling participle: The afternoon passed pleasantly, eating bon-bons and reading poetry. (Gwendolyn was doing this, but she is conspicuously absent from the sentence; therefore, the bon-bon eating and poetry reading was done by the afternoon as it passed by. Pleasantly.)

Dangling gerund: By walking a mile a day, her figure can be improved. ("Walking" does not refer to any word in this sentence. However, Gwendolyn can improve her figure by walking a mile a day and probably should.)

Dangling infinitive: To write good poetry, good poetry must be read. (The understood subject of "to write" must be the same as the subject of the sentence—in this case, "poetry." However, since Gwendolyn is the poet, clarity is achieved by making it "To write good poetry, Gwendolyn must read good poetry.")

Standard Lecture 61: Countersinking. Expositional redundancy, making the actions implied in a conversation explicit: e.g., "Let's get out here," he said, urging her to leave. Or, "I'm sorry," he said, apologizing to her. Or, "Why don't you go to bed with me?" he asked, making a play for her.

Standard Lecture 62: Speech-tag countersinking. This is a Said-Bookism that also attempts to make explicit that which is implicit. "Please forgive me," he apologized. It is not only lazy writing, but an indication that the author is not certain of the power of her own words so has to hammer them in a little harder.

Standard Lecture 63: This colon, like every colon throughout this ms. is a higher order of magnitude of punctuation than is required. In most places, a simple comma will do nicely; in others, an em-dash works very well. For no known reason, too many writers are in love with colons, and colons are the single most shocking—i.e., strongest—piece of punctuation there is and as such, must be used sparingly. Colons are like equal signs. They show the thoughts on both sides are identical. Semi-colons are like glue, so you can stick two independent clauses together for relationship emphasis. It seems to Mother Miller that there is a fad these days for throwing in colons at random, apparently under the mistaken notion that colons give that "high-tech" gloss to a piece, or perhaps under the equally mistaken idea that the use of a few colons can somehow salvage a poorly constructed sentence—winning through intimidation, she supposes. Wrong on all counts.

Standard Lecture 64: There is a difference between "lose" and "loose." Lose means to cease having something. Loose (*n.*) means to set something free. As an adjective, loose means free, and not fastened.

Standard Lecture 65: Tomato Surprise. Mainstay of the old Twilight Zone TV show. An entire pointless story—a conceit—contrived so the author can leap out of ambush to sling an overripe tomato into the face of the unsuspecting reader and then cry "Surprise! Fooled you!" There is a difference between a conceit and an idea. Good storytelling requires ideas, not conceits.

Standard Lecture 66: Deus Ex Machina. In ancient theater, when things got tense, the playwright was allowed to produce a Deus Ex Machina—literally, the god from the machine—to fly down on a wire provide a miraculous solution to an otherwise insoluble problem. This is no longer allowed. You can't solve your plot problems by saying, Look, the Martians all caught cold and died! even though Herbert George Wells did it and got away with it to boot. A subset of this writer-problem, the Deus-ette Ex Machina, occurs when, for example, everybody is trapped in a locked room and somebody discovers—just at the most convenient moment—he has the key in his pocket.

Standard Lecture 67: Infinite-verb phrase beginning sentence. This is a construction most beginners are inordinately fond of, for no known reason, and as such has come to typify amateur work and bad writing, especially in the minds of editors. Furthermore, two infinite-verb phrases denote concurrent activity when, in all likelihood, no such simultaneousness existed.

```
     Brushing the poodle and setting fire to
  his wastebasket, Stanley contemplated ordering
     lunch brought in.
```

This would be only a little better phrased as:

```
Brushing the poodle, Stanley contemplated
ordering lunch in. Moodily, he set fire to his
wastebasket.
```

Even better:

```
Stanley contemplated his deli order as he
brushed the poodle. He decided to forget lunch
and set fire to his wastebasket instead.
```

While the infinite-verb beginning phrase is technically correct in a grammatical sense, Mother Miller suggests re-doing the sentence anyway.

Standard Lecture 68: There are certain kinds of constructions that are sure tip-offs as to a writer's amateur status. Here are a few examples, culled and lightly edited from real sentences in real mss.:

```
Gwendolyn returned her gaze to the love
letter.
```
(Where had it been before, and what had it been doing while it was gone? Gwendolyn looked at the love letter again.)

```
When Stanley had finished his goodbye
waves to Harcourt and Cordelia he sat in a
chair until he had finished drinking martinis
and was called to dinner by Gwendolyn.
```
(Hat trick. "Finished" implies a finite task; waving goodbye is one, though goodbye waves aren't. Drinking martinis—especially when Stanley has to participate in wretched syntax like this—is not something one customarily thinks of as having been "finished." One may finish the martini one has at hand, however. Gwendolyn called him to dinner; this eliminates the abrupt shift into passive voice in the sentence. And where else would he sit? On the chandelier? Maybe he could occupy his favorite easy chair, but the wording in the sample sentence is simply ludicrous.)

>   After a moment, Stanley looked around
> himself and resumed kicking the poodle.

("After a moment" abounds in amateur writing; so does "looked around himself" and people "resuming" doing things. Stanley glanced around to see if anybody was looking and then kicked the poodle again.)

>   A rapid turn let Stanley land a good one
> squarely in little Fauntleroy's ribs.

(And what had been slowing Stanley down before now, not letting him do as he wished? Getting tangled in the dreadful syntax, Mother Miller must suppose. Stanley turned rapidly and landed a good one in little Fauntleroy's ribs as the wretched beast tried to run away.)

>   Gwendolyn stood in the doorway; she
> continued staring at Stanley for half an hour.

(If Gwendolyn were continuing to stare, that also indicates an ongoing activity—perhaps something she picks up at odd moments, like needlework—because as far as the text is concerned, she never began. Gwendolyn stood in the doorway staring at Stanley. Amateurs frequently have their characters stare at each other for precise lengths of time. The very thought makes Mother Miller's eyes burn.)

Standard Lecture 75: "To cross" is a transitive verb. It cannot stand alone, but must have an object (He crossed the room) or a predicate nominative (The dirty rat went and crossed me) and must not be used as an intransitive verb (He crossed to the window). The prepositional phrase (to the window) does not serve as object for the verb. It is used this way in stage directions (First and Second Villains cross and exeunt stage r., laughing), but that is stage jargon shorthand with the object understood (. . .cross [stage] and exeunt. . .) and definitely isn't prose writing.

Standard Lecture 79: This word is a proper adjective—i.e., it comes from a proper noun. While some proper adjectives have passed into such common use capitalization is no longer considered necessary, this one has not yet achieved that status and must be capitalized—

other examples are Latin lover, Roman nose, Greek fire, Scotch whiskey, French pastry, etc. On the other hand, "bourbon" seems to have achieved non-capitalization status.

Standard Lecture 83: "It's" is not the possessive form of the indefinite singular pronoun. "It's" means "it is"; therefore, when you write, "The cat was licking it's fur", what you are saying is: "The cat was licking it is fur." Conversely, "its" cannot be used when "it is" is intended.

Standard Lecture 91: Names. This one sounds wrong. The naming of names, as T.S. Eliot said, is a very important thing. The use of common, everyday and contemporary names in a work set elsewhere, such as in a foreign land, or another time or place, comes as a shock jarring enough to shake the reader out of the dream whenever one of these names is encountered. A name is evocative of the character who bears it; for example, a Maggie is a far different sort from a Margaret.

Standard Lecture 97: Name-calling. When an author has her characters addressing each other by name, this is usually a dead giveaway that he is spoon-feeding information—usually to the VPC, who is lurking about, listening, and it would be convenient for everyone to know who is speaking to whom. But how many times do you really call someone by name when you are talking to him? Try it, for drill. You'll quickly realize how artificial it sounds. And it reads much worse.

Standard Lecture 98: Disconnected Body Parts (DBP). Hands, arms, legs, eyes, or any other part of the anatomy do not often operate independently of their owner; such is the case here, where the character is using this DBP as a tool. Beware of scattering DBPs through your text, as it is both messy and misleading. If you have little feet running along a path in the woods, for example, even though you, the author, may know very well what is happening and who is doing the running, the reader does not. It could be a squirrel, a small person, an insect, a lizard or a rat attached to those little feet that, apparently, now move all by their own lone selves. In such a case, not only has the author committed the dreaded DBP error, but he is also indulging in mystification.

Essay Eighteen:
A Brief Listing of Grammatical Terms

Note: This essay is not to be confused with a thorough exploration and examination of grammar! This is intended as a quick reference only.

Absolute Phrase. An Absolute Phrase is one that is grammatically independent but closely related in meaning to the rest of the sentence. It is a rather formal construction not often found in informal writing. A Nominative Absolute consists of a noun or a pronoun followed by a participle.

```
The polo match having ended, Gwendolyn
went home.
```
Abstract Noun. See Noun.
Active Voice. See Voice.
Adjective. A part of speech used to modify (i.e., describe or limit.] a noun or noun substitute.
Descriptive adjectives:
    blue sky, good will, American citizen, waving flag, elaborate preparations, snooty salesperson
Limiting adjectives:
    Possessive: my cat, its dish, their homes
Demonstrative:
    this idea, that one, these men, those polo ponies
Interrogative:
    Whose cap? Which one? What ball gown?
Indefinite:
    some money, more effort, several others, many poodles
Numerical:
    one pear tree, three French hens, first robin, third base, twentieth anniversary

Adjective Clause. A subordinate clause used as an adjective.
> The gentleman who is honest will succeed.

[The clause, equivalent to the adjective *honest*, modifies the noun *gentleman*.]

Adverb. A part of speech used to modify a word [or word group] other than a noun or pronoun. An adverb may qualify or limit a verb, an adjective, another adverb, or even a whole clause. An adverb often indicates time [are now going], place [stayed there], manner [acting quickly], or degree [very eager].

> Stand here. [*Here* modifies the verb *stand*.]
> Stand beside the very nice gazebo. [*Very* modifies the adjective *nice*.]
> Stand very quietly. [*Very* modifies the adverb *quietly*, which modifies the verb *stand*.]
> Certainly you may be seated. [*Certainly* modifies the main clause.]

Adverb Clause. A subordinate clause used as an adverb.

> I shall leave the gazebo after Gwendolyn comes. [The adverb clause *after Gwendolyn comes* modifies the verb *shall leave* and indicates time. Adverb clauses may also indicate place, manner, cause, purpose, condition, concession, comparison, or result.]

Agreement. The correspondence in form of one word with another [such as a verb with its subject, or a pronoun with its antecedent] to indicate person and number.

Antecedent. The name given to a word of group of words to which a pronoun refers.

> This is the man who came to the house. [*Man* is the antecedent of the relative pronoun *who*.]
> When Stanley and Gwendolyn came, they told us the good news. [*Stanley and Gwendolyn* are the antecedents of the personal pronoun *they*.]

Appositive. A noun or noun substitute set beside another noun or noun substitute and identifying or explaining it.

> Dr. Pain, our orthodontist, is visiting England, his native country. [*Orthodontist* is in apposition with *Dr. Pain*, and *country* is in apposition with *England*.]

Article. The definite article *the* and the indefinite articles *a* and *an* are usually classified as adjectives. They indicate that a noun or noun substitute is to follow.

Auxiliary. A word that is used to form various tenses of verbs. *Have, may, can, be, shall, will, must, should* and *do* are common auxiliaries.

```
I shall go.
He was sent away.
He has been promoted.
```

Case. The inflection form of a noun [man's] or pronoun [he, his, him] to show such relations as subject [subjective or nominative case—he], possession [possessive case—man's, his], or object [objective case—him].

Clause. A group of words that contains a verb and its subject and is used as part of a sentence. A clause may be main [independent, principal] or subordinate [dependent].

(1) A main [independent, principal] clause can stand by itself as a simple sentence.

```
The poodle barked and the kitten washed
his paws.  [Two main clauses, either of which can stand by itself
as a simple sentence.]
```

(2) A subordinate [dependent] clause cannot stand alone. It is used as a noun, an adjective, or an adverb.

```
That Stanley will run for office is doubtful.  [Noun clause: a
subordinate clause used as subject of the sentence.]
```

Collective Noun. See Noun.

Colloquial. Appropriate for conversation and informal writing rather than for formal writing.

Common Noun. See Noun.

Comparison. The change in the form of an adjective or adverb to indicate degrees of superiority in quality, quantity, or manner. There are three degrees: positive, comparative, and superlative.

EXAMPLES:

Positive	*Comparative*	*Superlative*
good	better	best
high	higher	highest
quickly	more quickly	most quickly

Complement. A word or words used to complete the sense of the verb, the subject, or the object. The complement may be an object, a predicate noun, or a predicate adjective.

OBJECTS:

> Stanley gave the poodle a swift kick. [*Kick* is the direct object, *poodle* is the indirect object despite being the direct recipient of the kick. To put it another way, Stanley gave a swift kick to Fauntleroy.]

PREDICATE NOUNS:

> Fauntleroy was a spoiled poodle. [The predicate noun poodle, referring to the subject Fauntleroy, is also called the predicate complement, the subjective complement, or the predicate nominative.]

> He called the man a bum. [*Man* is the direct object. The noun *bum*, referring to man, is called the objective complement or the predicate complement.]

PREDICATE ADJECTIVES:

> The poodle is disobedient. [The predicate adjective *disobedient*, referring to the subject *poodle*, is also called the subjective complement or the predicate complement.]

> Gwendolyn dyed Fauntleroy blue. [*Fauntleroy* is the direct object. The predicate adjective *blue*, referring to Fauntleroy, is also called the objective complement or the predicate objective.]

Complete Predicate. See Predicate.

Complete Subject. See Subject.

Complex Sentence. See Sentence.

Compound Sentence. See Sentence.

Compound-complex Sentence. See Sentence.

Concrete Noun. See Noun.

Conjugation. A grouping of verb forms to indicate tense, voice, mood, number, and person. See also Inflection.

Conjunction. A part of speech (often called a function word) used to connect words, phrases, or clauses. There are two kinds; co-ordinating conjunctions and subordinating conjunctions.

(1) Co-ordinating conjunctions connect words, phrases, and clauses of equal rank: *and, but, or, nor, for* and sometimes *so* and *yet*.

(2) Subordinating conjunctions connect subordinate clauses with

main clauses: *if, although, since, in order that, as, because, unless, after, before, until, when, whenever, where, while, wherever,* etc.

Conjunctive Adverb. An adverb which can also be used to connect or relate main clauses: *however, therefore, nevertheless, hence, than, besides, moreover, thus, otherwise, consequently, accordingly,* etc.

Construction. See Syntax.

Co-ordinate, co-ordinating. Of equal rank. For example, two nouns, two infinitives, or two main clauses.

Copula (Copulative verb). See Linking verb.

Declension. See Inflection.

Demonstrative Adjective. See Adjective.

Demonstrative Pronoun. See Pronoun.

Dependent Clause. See Clause.

Descriptive Adjective. See Adjective.

Diagramming. An arrangement of words on lines to show relationships within the sentence. Various forms are used and can be found in many good grammar books. Any form is serviceable if it help the user understand the sentence. A diagram is only a means to an end, not an end in itself.

Direct Address (Nominative of address, vocative). A noun or pronoun used parenthetically to direct a speech to a definite person.

```
I hope, Gwendolyn, that you will go.
Stanley, close the door.
```

Direct Object. See Object.

Direct Quotations. The exact oral or written words of others.

Direct quotation:
```
Stanley asked, "Why don't you join us,
Gwendolyn?"
```
Indirect quotation:
```
Stanley asked Gwendolyn why she didn't
join the group.
```

Ellipsis (Elliptical expression). An expression in which words are omitted but which is nonetheless clear because the omitted words can be readily supplied.

```
Gwendolyn is prettier than Cordelia [is
pretty].
```

>   Whenever [it is] possible, you should eat
> bon-bons.

Use the Ellipsis Mark [three spaced periods] to indicate an omission of one or more words within a quoted passage. If the omission ends with a period (End Ellipsis), use four spaced periods (one to mark the end of the sentence and three to show the omission). An ellipsis takes no other punctuation.

Expletive. *It* or *there* used merely as an introductory word or filler.
>   It is true that he is not coming.
>   There were few poodles present.

Finite Verb. A verb or verb form that makes a complete assertion and may thus serve as a predicate.
>   "The sun rose."
>   "The sun is rising."

Infinitives, participles, and gerunds are Verbals, not Finite Verbs.

Form Change. See Inflection.Gerund Phrase. See Phrase.

Idiom. An expression in good use that is peculiar to a language. (Idioms sometimes violate established rules of grammar, but are nevertheless sanctioned by usage.)
>   I have known Stanley for many a year.
>   I am not myself today.

Imperative. See Mood.

Indefinite Pronoun. See Pronoun.

Independent Clause (Main clause, principal clause). See Clause.

Independent Element. Any word or group of words that has no grammatical connection with the rest of the sentence.

Direct Address
>   I hope, Harcourt, that you can go.

Interpolation
>   The whole family, we hope, will come.

Absolute Expression
>   Darkness having come, Harcourt slipped
> away.

Interjection
>   Ah, polo is the sport I enjoy.

Indicative. See Mood.

Indirect Object. See Object.
Indirect Quotation. See Direct quotation.
Infinitive. See Verbals.
Infinitive Phrase. See Phrase.
Inflection. A change in the form of a word to show a change in meaning or in grammatical relationship to some other word or group of words. The inflection of nouns and pronouns is called declension; the inflection of verbs, conjugation; that of adjectives and adverbs, comparison.

Inflection of Verbs (indicating tense, person, mood)
```
look, looking, looks, looked, looked
drink, drinking, drinks, drank, drunk
know, knowing, knows, knew, known
be, being, am, is, are, was, were, been
```
Inflection of Nouns (indicating number, case)
```
dog, dogs, dog's, dogs'
child, children, child's, children's
```
Inflection of Pronouns (indicating case, person, number)
```
I, me, my, mine, we, us, our, ours
who, whom, whose, someone, someone's
This is old. These are old. That is older
```
than those.
Inflection of Modifiers (indicating comparison, number)
```
fast, faster, fastest, bad, worse, worst
attractive, more attractive, most
```
attractive
```
this letter, these letters, that letter,
```
those letters

Intensive Pronoun. See Pronoun.
Interjection. A part of speech expressing emotion and having no grammatical relation with other words in the sentence.
```
Oh, I can hardly believe it.
Whew! That was a narrow escape.
```
Interrogative Pronoun. See Pronoun.
Intransitive. See Verb.
Irregular Verb. See Strong verb.
Limiting Adjective. See Adjective.
Linking Verb. A verb used to express the relationship between the subject and the predicate noun or predicate adjective. The chief

linking verbs are be, become, seem, appear, and verbs pertaining to the senses.

```
He is brave. I feel bad. Harcourt became a
lawyer.
```

Main Clause (Independent clause). See Clause.

Modifier. Any word or group of words that describes or qualifies another word or group of words. See Modify.

Modify. To describe or qualify the meaning of a word or group of words.

```
A very dirty poodle romped gaily beside
the gazebo.
```
[*A* and *dirty* modify *poodle*; *very* modifies *dirty*; *gaily* and *beside the gazebo* modify *romped*; *the* modifies *gazebo*.]

See also Inflection.

Mood (Mode). The form of the verb that is used to indicate the manner in which the action or state is conceived. English has indicative, imperative, and subjunctive moods.

The indicative mood states a fact or asks a question.

```
You have a good mind. Have you any ideas?
Gwendolyn is here. Is Cordelia here?
```

The imperative mood gives a command, makes a request, or gives directions.

```
Be careful. Watch your step, please. Take
the next number and wait your turn patiently,
please.
```

The subjunctive mood expresses a doubt, a condition contrary to fact, a wish or regret, a concession, a supposition.

```
I wish that Gwendolyn were here.
If I had my way, you would not go.
Were it not so, Gwendolyn would have
forgiven Stanley.
If this be treason, make the most of it.
```

Nominative. Equivalent to Subjective. See Case.

Nominative Absolute. See Absolute phrase.

Nominative of Address. See Direct address.

Nonrestrictive Modifier. A nonessential modifier. A parenthetical phrase or clause which does not identify the person or thing modified. See also Restrictive Modifier.

Noun. A part of speech (name of a person, place, thing, quality, or action) that usually changes form to make the possessive case and the plural (poodle, poodle's, poodles). See also Inflection.

Nouns are used as:

1. Subjects of verbs (The *poodle* yapped.)
2. Objects of verbs (Stanley opened the door to let the poodle out of the gazebo.)
3. Predicate nouns (He was *Gwendolyn*'s pet.)
4. Appositives (Hortense, *Gwendolyn's friend*, is allergic to poodles.)
5. Nominatives of address (*Stanley*, quit kicking Fauntleroy.)
6. Predicate objectives/Objective complements (*Gwendolyn* called Stanley a bully.)

Nouns are classified as:

1. Common—applied to persons, places, or things (man, woman, peacock, poodle, city, country, gazebo).
2. Proper—applied to a specific individual, place, or thing (Stanley Wanderlust, Harcourt P. Dweeb, South Yellowstone, the Colossus of Rhodes, the Golden Gate Bridge).
3. Collective—applied to a group (troupe, gang, bunch, pod, kindle, herd, division, squad).
4. Concrete—applied to something discernable by one or more of the senses (lion, cage, blank gun, chair).
5. Abstract—applied to a quality or general idea (fear, love, bravery, cowardice).

Noun Clause. A subordinate clause used as a noun. It may be used as subject, direct object, appositive, predicate nominative, object of a preposition.

```
Whoever comes will be welcome at the
party. (Subject)
    I hope that Gwendolyn will get over her
headache. (Object of the Verb)
    The hope that he might win upheld Stanley
in the polo match. (Appositive)
    This is what Gwendolyn was hoping for.
(Predicate)
    I shall invest Gwendolyn's lottery
winnings in whatever get-rich scheme seems
best. (Object of preposition in)
```

Noun Substitute. A pronoun or any group of words such as a gerund phrase, an infinitive phrase, or a noun clause, that functions as a noun. See also Substantive.

Number. The change in the form of a word—noun, pronoun, etc.—to designate one (singular) or more than one (plural). See also Inflection.

Object. A noun, pronoun or noun substitute that follows and completes the meaning of a transitive verb or follows a preposition.

Direct Object: Any noun or equivalent that answers the question What? or Whom? after a transitive verb. Direct objects ordinarily receive, or in some way are affected by, the action of the verb.

```
Harcourt punched Stanley. Stanley knew why
Harcourt had hit him.
```

Indirect Object: Any noun or equivalent that is indirectly affected by the action of the verb, and that states to whom or for whom something is done.

```
Stanley gave Fauntleroy a dirty look.
```
(*look* is the direct object, *Fauntleroy* the indirect object, of the verb *gave*. It is usually possible to substitute for the indirect object a prepositional phrase with *to* or *for*. Stanley gave a dirty look to Fauntleroy.)

Object of a Preposition: Any noun or equivalent following a preposition. (See Preposition.)

```
Gwendolyn drifted into the gazebo.
```
(*gazebo* is the object of the preposition *into*.)

Objective Complement. See Complement.

Participial Phrase. See Phrase.

Participle. See Verbals.

Parts of Speech. The eight classes into which most grammarians group words according to their form changes and/or their uses in the sentence: verb, noun, pronoun, adjective, adverb, conjunction, preposition, and interjection. It is important to note that part of speech is determined by function. The same word is often used as several different parts of speech.

Passive Voice. See Voice.

Person. Changes in the form of verbs and pronouns which indicate whether a person is speaking (first person), is spoken to (second person), or is spoken about (third person).

First Person
> I see Stanley.

Second Person
> Can you see Stanley?

Third Person
> He sees Stanley.

Personal Pronoun. See Pronoun.

Phrase. A group of related words which lacks subject and verb and is used as a single part of speech.

Prepositional Phrase:
> The man with red hair is Harcourt.

[Adjective]
> Harcourt lives in the city. [Adverb]

Participial Phrase:
> The door leading to the gazebo is open.

[Adjective]

Gerund Phrase:
> Playful kittens romping in gazebos are responsible for many giggles. [Noun substitute]

Infinitive Phrase:
> To err is human. [Noun substitute]

Verb Phrases:
> Harcourt has been unemployed for a year.

[Verb]

See also Verb and Verbals.

Predicate. The part of the sentence comprising what is said about the subject. The Complete Predicate consists of the verb (the Simple Predicate) along with its complements and modifiers.

> Stanley runs through the gazebo. [*Runs* is the simple predicate; *runs through the gazebo* is the complete predicate.]

Predicate Adjective, Predicate Complement, Predicate Nominative, Predicate Noun, Predicate Objective. See Complement.

Preposition. A part of speech (often called a function word) that is used to show the relation of a noun or that of a noun—equivalent to some other word in the sentence.

> The gazebo is in the garden. [The preposition *in* shows the relationship of the noun *gazebo* to the verb *is*.]

Across, after, at, before, between, by, for, from, in, of, on, over, under, *with*, *up*, and *near* are commonly used prepositions.

Prepositional Phrase. See Phrase.

Principal Clause (Main clause, Independent clause). See Clause.

Principal Parts. The forms of any verb from which the various tenses are derived: (1) present stem (infinitive), (2) past tense, and (3) past participle.

EXAMPLES:

see	saw	seen
take	took	taken
love	loved	loved

Progressive Verb. A form of the verb (ending in -ing and following a part of the auxiliary be) used to express continuous action or state of being.

```
Gwendolyn was moping in the gazebo.
I have been playing polo all afternoon.
```

Pronoun. A part of speech used instead of a noun.

Personal pronouns: I, you, he, she, etc. (See also Case.)

Interrogative pronouns: who, which, what

```
Who is he?
```

Relative pronouns: who, which, that

```
He who steals my purse steals trash.
```

Demonstrative pronouns: this, that, these, those

```
This is more useful than that.
```

Indefinite pronouns: each, either, any, anyone, some, someone, no one, few, all, everyone, etc.

Reciprocal pronouns: myself, yourself, himself, etc.

```
I blamed myself.
```

Intensive pronouns: myself, yourself, himself, etc.

```
I myself will go.
```

See also Inflection.

Proper Adjective. An adjective formed from a proper noun, as Spanish from Spain.

Proper Noun. See Noun.

Quotation. See Direct quotation.

Reciprocal Pronoun. See Pronoun.

Reflexive Pronoun. See Pronoun.

Regular Verb. See Weak verb.

Relative Pronoun. See Pronoun.

Restrictive Modifier. An essential modifier. A phrase or clause which identifies the word modified and which therefore cannot be omitted without changing the essential meaning of the sentence.

```
Any person who talks incessantly is a
bore.
```

See also Nonrestrictive Modifier.

Sentence. A unit of expression that may stand alone. A grammatically complete sentence contains at least a verb (predicate) and its subject (one or the other sometimes implied), with or without modifiers. Sentences are classified structurally as (1) simple, (2) compound, (3) complex, or (4) compound-complex.

(1) Simple sentence. A sentence containing but one main clause and no subordinate clauses.

Five basic patterns of the simple sentence:

1. Subject-Verb

```
The women are singing happily.
The horses were led to the water.
```

2. Subject-Verb-Direct Object

```
I forgot my assignment.
```

3. SUBJECT-VERB-INDIRECT OBJECT-DIRECT OBJECT

```
Gwendolyn mailed me a birthday gift.
```

4. Subject-Linking Verb-Predicate Adjective

```
Recently she appears very unhappy.
```

5. Subject-Linking Verb-Predicate Noun

```
She may be a famous actress some day.
```

Simple sentences may have compound subjects, verbs, objects, etc.

```
Gwendolyn and Hortense sing and dance.
```

(2) Compound sentence. A sentence containing two or more main clauses but no subordinate clauses.

```
The peacock screeched and the poodle
yapped.
```

(3) Complex sentence. A sentence containing one main clause and one or more subordinate clauses.

```
    Poodles yap [main clause] when they are startled
[subordinate clause].
```

(4) Compound-complex sentence. A sentence containing two or more main clauses and one or more subordinate clauses.

```
Seagulls clamored [main clause 1] overhead and
a bomb fell [main clause 2] where we had stood
[subordinate clause].
```

Simple Predicate. See Predicate.
Simple Sentence. See Sentence.
Simple Subject. See Subject.
Strong Verb (Irregular Verb). A verb that forms its principal parts in various ways other than by the addition of *-ed*, *-d*, or *-t*. See also Inflection.

EXAMPLES

Vowel changes:
swim, swam, swum
Addition of -en:
beat, beat, beaten
No change:
set, set, set

Subject. The person or thing (in a sentence or clause) about which an assertion is made. The subject and the words associated with it make up the Complete Subject.

```
The poodle coming out of the gazebo barked
at the peacock. [poodle is the Simple Subject; the poodle
coming out of the gazebo is the Complete Subject.]
```

Subjunctive. See Case.
Subjective Complement. See Complement.
Subjunctive. See Mood.
Subordinate Clause. A dependent clause. See Clause.
Substantive. Any word or group of words used as a noun. Substantives may be nouns, pronouns, phrases (especially gerund or infinitive phrases, or noun clauses.
Syntax (Construction). Sentence structure. The grammatical function of words, phrases, clauses.
Tense. Change in the form of the verb to indicate time. See Inflection.
Transitive. See Verb.
Verb. A part of speech that is used to assert action or being and

that changes form to indicate time, person, mood. See Inflection.

Transitive verb. A verb either passive in form (see Voice) or requiring a direct object to complete its meaning. See Object.

    `Stanley kicked Gwendolyn's poodle.`

Intransitive Verb. A verb not having an object and not passive in form. See Voice.

    `I was in Venezuela last Christmas.`
    `She has been waiting patiently for hours.`

Verb Phrase. See Phrase.

Verbals. Words derived from verbs but used as nouns or adjectives (or sometimes as adverbs). The three verbals are Gerunds, Participles, Infinitives.

The Gerund is used only as a noun and always ends in -ing. It may be used as subject (`Swimming is fun`), as object of a verb (`I enjoy swimming`), as object of a preposition (`By swimming he reached shore`), or as an appositive (`My chief recreation is swimming`). The gerund, like a noun, may be modified by an adjective (`Skillful swimming saved his life`). The gerund shows its verbal origin by its ability to take an object (`Swimming a choppy stream can be dangerous`) or to be modified by an adverb (`By swimming rapidly, he escaped`).

The Participle is used only as an adjective. Because the present participle ends in *-ing*, it can be distinguished from the gerund only by its use in the sentence.

    `Swimming is fun.` [Gerund—a noun, subject of the verb is.]

    `A swimming suit is needed.` [Participle—an adjective modifying the noun suit.]

Participles: the rising sun, a concealed weapon, a lost cause, a broken bone, a bone broken by a fall, a worn coat, a coat worn by a beggar. [Note the varying endings of the past participle—*ed, -t, -en*—and the internal shifts in worn (from wear).]

The Infinitive is used chiefly as a noun, less frequently as an adjective or an adverb. It is made up of *to* plus a verb, but after certain verbs, this too may be omitted:

    `He helped (to) make the kite.`
    `He dared not (to) go away.`

Used As a Noun
>   To walk was a pleasure. [Subject]
>   He began to open the box. [Object of verb]
>   Her wish was to see him leave. [Predicate noun]
>   I will do anything except (to) groom the poodle. [Object of preposition]

Used As an Adjective
>   I have work to do. [*To do* modifies the noun *work*]

Used As an Adverb
>   He enlisted to become an astronaut. [The infinitive modifies the verb *enlisted*.]

The infinitive shows its verbal origin by its ability to take a subject (I asked him to go), to take an object (I wanted to pay him), or to be modified by an adverb (I asked him to drive slowly). Note that the subject of the infinitive is in the objective case.

Vocative. See Direct address.

Voice. Distinction in the form of a verb to indicate whether the subject acts (active voice) or is acted upon (passive voice).
>   Gwendolyn ate the bon-bon. [Active voice; the subject, *Gwendolyn*, acts on the object, the *bon-bon*.]
>   The bon-bon was eaten by Gwendolyn. [Passive voice; the subject, the bon-bon, was acted on by the predicate nominative, Gwendolyn.]

Weak Verb (Regular Verb). Any verb that forms its principal parts by adding *-ed, -d,* or *-t* to the infinitive: love, loved, loved; sweep, swept, swept.

Essay Nineteen:
Sit and Set, Lie and Lay

These two sets of verbs are the most vile and wretched in the English language because they are frequently confused because of their similarities in spelling or meaning. They may share the same forms, but the meaning is different according to context.

LIE (to recline, Intransitive)
lay   lain   lying

LAY (to cause to lie, Transitive)
laid   laid   laying

SIT (to be seated, Intransitive)
sat   sat   sitting

SET (to place or put, Transitive)
set   set   setting

    Wrong: He lay the book on the table. [Past tense of the transitive verb lay needed]
    Right: He laid the book on the table.
    Right: The book is lying (not laying) on the table.
    Wrong: He set in the chair. [Past tense of the intransitive verb sit needed]
    Right: He sat in the chair.
    Right: He set the bucket on the table. [Transitive]
    Right: The man is sitting (not setting) in the chair.

Essay Twenty:
Clay Feet

By now, Gentle Reader, being the clever and observant sort referenced at the beginning of our journey together, has probably figured out the rest of the title of this work—that How To Write Good means how to teach oneself how to write good prose, good dialogue, and one can hope, use these skills to write good short stories, articles and novels.

But, Gentle Reader says with a certain understandable plaintiveness, I can always spot the flaws in somebody else's work. And sometimes I can even suggest fairly good ways to fix these flaws. Why am I not perfect by now?

You've discovered the catch. The secret. Here it is, in ever-so-soft a voice lest anybody else overhear:

```
We all have trouble
doing as we say and
not as we do 100% of
the time!!!
```

Ignore the stacked punctuation. It was necessary just this once.

Do you think any of us like having our compatriots catch us with our participle dangling (trust Mother Miller, they love it. Relish it, even). Do you think we enjoy losing our antecedent one more time? Do you think we have fun when the dialogue we could hear so clearly in our heads, with differing voices saying the lines, can't be untangled because we forgot to leave clues as to which was doing the talking when and/or to whom? Do you think we are amused when the scene that is so vivid on the undersides of our eyelids fails to be transmitted to another reader and he complains that he hasn't a clue as to what the place looks like? And so on, ad nauseam.

Attempting to master that wonderful, contrary thing, the English language, is something we who would write must do. I have a deep and abiding love for the language; our mother tongue will endure long after all those who today can't tell an adverb from an adjective (or care about the difference) have passed from this Earth. It will survive the deliberate destructive efforts of the deconstructionists, the atrocities committed upon it by the ignorant, the mayhem inflicted by the purveyors of shoddy goods. Nevertheless, when I see it misused, and especially by those who must be the banner-carriers of good and clear usage—the writers and would-be writers among us—I fly into my whitest of armor, take up my sword, and do battle.

When we fail—and we frequently do—all we can do is stagger back to the keyboard, or quill and inkwell, or whatever our favorite form of torture is, and give it one more try, hoping this time for the clarity we seek.

Welcome to the club.

Principal Parts of Verbs

Present stem	Past tense	Past participle
begin	began	begun
bite	bit	bitten
blow	blew	blown
break	broke	broken
bring	brought	brought
burst	burst	burst
catch	caught	caught
choose	chose	chosen
come	came	come
dive	1) dived, 2) dove	dived
do	did	done
drag	dragged	dragged
draw	drew	drawn
drink	drank	drunk
eat	ate	eaten
fall	fell	fallen
fly	flew	flown
freeze	froze	frozen
get	got	1) got, 2) gotten
give	gave	given
go	went	gone
grow	grew	grown
hang (execute)	hanged	hanged
hang (suspend)	hung	hung
know	knew	known
lead	led	led
lie (falsify)	lied	lied
lose	lost	lost
raise	raised	raised
ride	rode	ridden
rise	rose	risen
run	ran	run
shine (radiate)	shone	shone

Present stem	Past tense	Past participle
shine (polish)	shined	shined
shrink	1) shrank, 2) shrunk	shrunk
sing	1) sang, 2) sung	sung
sink	1) sank, 2) sunk	sunk
sneak	sneaked	sneaked
speak	spoke	spoken
spring	1) sprang, 2) sprung	sprung
steal	stole	stolen
swim	swam	swum
swing	swung	swung
take	took	taken
tear	tore	torn
throw	threw	thrown
wear	wore	worn
weave	wove	woven
wreak	wrought	1) wrought, 2) wreaked
write	wrote	written

```
Your Legal Name                          Approximately ?000 words
Your Address                             (to nearest 500)
Your City, State, Zip
Phone: (555)555-5555
Fax:   (555)555-5555
Email: name@service.com




(Space down approximately to the middle of the page--and don't put
this instruction on your ms.! This space is necessary for the editor
to use to jot down notes of various sorts concerning what to do with
the story when she buys it.)



                              Title
                          by Your Name

     This is a standard, workable, short story ms. format. Opening
line goes as above, where you also start double-spacing. Once upon a
time. It really was a dark and stormy night. Suddenly a shot rang
out and the butler dropped dead, quite surprised to be the victim for
a change.
     "Your legal name," above, is the way you want the check made out.
The by-line name may be entirely different. Don't worry about editors
sorting it out; they do it all the time. Do not put your title in
all-capital letters. They must be marked for lower case, and you do
not want to give somebody a free excuse to touch your ms. with a
writing utensil.
     Use a one-inch margin on the top, bottom and sides, and double-
space the text. Justify the left margin only. Do not number the
first page of a short story, but use a header spaced within the one-
```

Addendum on Manuscript Style

*This section is one on ms. preparation and contains a lot of really good information concerning the appearance of manuscript pages–but manuscript pages are physically larger than this book. Therefore, Mother Miller asks you kindly to pretend that the pages are standard 8-1/2x11 with one-inch borders all around instead, instead of being scaled down. An Acrobat **PDF** file of the full-size pages is available at www.foxacre.com/pageform.htm. Thank you ever so much.*

```
YourLastName                          Identifying Word / Page 2
```

inch top margin on the next and subsequent pages:

```
    YourLastName                          Identifying Word/Page #
```

Note that the header is approximately a half inch from the top of the paper so if a photocopy is made, it won't get inadvertently dropped out, and that there are three blank lines between the header and the body copy; this is for clarity's sake and is easy to do by entering the proper codes in the header itself. Use Old Courier, by preference, 12-pt. Please don't use teeny-tiny type unless you are dealing with an editor you never want to sell to. If you are using that wretched, much too light New Courier, try setting the ms. itself in bold type while leaving the header in regular. Eats up toner, but it's easier for the editor to read and she might even notice the extra effort you went to. In any event, it's a grace note you might want to consider, nothing more, and not a hard-and-fast rule.

Some editors get cranky about just what goes just where, but this header format will carry you through most ms. situations. In general, you want to put the most important information--the word that identifies your story, what page--where it is most accessible to the person whipping through the ms., and that's at the top right-hand corner. If the editor wants to know more, such as who has written this wonderful thing he is reading, he will glance over toward the left.

The reason you must maintain the one inch all around is if you gum up the margins, you also gum up the editor's means of calculating word counts (and she doesn't care that your word processor counts words--she has her own methods, thanks). Pica type is preferable, but elite is acceptable. The overwhelming majority of editors want mss. done the old-fashioned way--white paper, double-spaced 12-pt.

Courier type. Boring--but readable. Do <u>not</u> manually double-space! Do <u>not</u> double-space between paragraphs and skip indentation! <u>Do</u> use a five-space indent at the start of each paragraph. <u>Do</u> use only one side of the paper!

   Some programs will give you line-and-a-half spacing; don't even think about it because this is even more difficult to read than single space and trying to figure word count simply infuriates editors and causes them to curse your name. Another sure-fire way to turn an editor against you for life is to use proportional typeface. All the word-count formulae go right out the window. Also, you ever try to carat in a missing letter in a proportionally spaced word? Use clean, white paper and fresh ink in your ribbons if you're using an impact printer. Black ribbons. If you are using an ink-jet printer, beware of over-inking. Make sure your toner cartridge isn't dying if you use a laser printer.

   If you still hand-type, do not use erasable bond; it is slippery and tends to fly all over an editor's office at the slightest provocation. It also smudges badly during the editing process. Most professional writers use plain old copy bond.

   Do <u>not</u> send your only copy of anything to anybody! You'd be amazed at how many people commit this blunder, though editors see it all the time.

   In your text, don't use capitals for emphasis. And do be sparing of italics or other typographical gim-crackery. Clean, uncluttered text is what you're after. If your word processor can make real italics, don't do it. This annoys editors and puzzles typesetters, who are used to seeing italics underlined. If, in spite of everything, you have to have a long passage in italics, don't underline the whole thing. Draw a pencil line down the left margin and write "ital" beside it. When you do wish to indicate italics, <u>make the underline connect the words,</u> not <u>interrupt</u> <u>and</u> <u>underline</u> <u>word</u> <u>by</u> <u>word</u>. If you have to jiggle with your word processor for an hour to make it do this, it's good enough for you, she said heartlessly.

Do not break words with hyphens at the end of lines and avoid ending a line with a legitimate hyphen if you can possibly avoid it, such as in the word "mother-in-law", even if your word processor is kind enough to do it for you. Hyphens at the ends of lines also annoy editors who must mark them, and puzzle typesetters, who don't know quite what to do with them. Typesetters don't need any help from you in creating typographical errors.

You might notice the lone line at the bottom or top of some of the pages in this piece; you should leave these lines, called widows or orphans, in mss. Disable the feature you might have on your word processor that suppresses widow and orphan lines. This will, cumulatively, also gum up word counts by throwing the overall page count off for those editors who reckon the weight by that method.

Here's a brief way to calculate word count. Take the number of characters per average, mid-paragraph line, divided by 6, times lines per page times number of pages, and correct for fraction pages at the beginning and end. Do not take your word processor's count; it will cheat you.

If you have left out a word or a letter in a word and it's too late to re-do the page, insert a carat-mark (^) at the proper place and write in the missing item <u>in pencil</u>. You may decide later to correct your correction, you see, and it's easier all around if you do it this way. In these days of computers there is no excuse for sending out a ms. with corrected errors in it unless you are bumping up, hard, against a deadline. There is little excuse for this if you

YourLastName   Identifying Word / Page 5

are hand-typing your work. If there is more than one correction per
page or more than two per ten pages of ms., you have to re-type it.
So stop sniveling, get to it, and resolve to be more careful next
time.

You must read your work even though you have run it through the
spelling checker, to catch New Age typos--the ones that make real
words and won't set off bells. Also, a few publishers are accepting
work on diskette these days, and if you rely on someone else to fix
your typos, you're in for a rude awakening. As if that weren't
enough, you will, at one time or another, encounter somebody who can
neither spell nor punctuate. The days of letting somebody else take
care of boring little details like this are over.

Scene breaks, as opposed to chapter sections, are indicated by
a blank line, number-sign centered, blank line in the body of the
text, as follows:

#

This informs editor and typesetter that the extra lines are in
there deliberately, and not because you or your word processor had
the hiccups.

This writer likes to break chapters of a novel into sections,
headed by small Roman numerals. In a short story, however, she uses
the simple but elegant arrangement described above.

If you use a computer, you can take the standard spacing of
first-page elements, down to the by-line, including the header codes
your word processor requires, re-do them to reflect your own name
and address, phone number, fax number, etc., and transfer this setup
to a permanent template or format file, presupposing you are using a
MS-DOS computer. If not, do whatever your own system requires along
these lines. Once you have it, you can then call it up whenever you

YourLastName   Identifying Word / Page 6

need it, edit it to fit, and carry on.

Do not use a cover page for a short story. Do not staple the pages; a simple paper clip is useful but not mandatory. Mail it flat and make sure it stays that way as it undergoes the tender mercies of the Post Awful by stiffening the envelope with a piece of cardboard. Cover letters are nice but not required as the editor who receives your ms. can probably guess that you want him to read it. If you enclose a cover letter, do keep it dignified. No groveling, no threats. No fancy hand-done illustrations with cute elves, or glaring paper colors. (As an editor I once got a cover letter on Day-Glo orange paper. No joke. Big headache.) Nowadays, with postal rates being what they are and going up all the time, it's become standard practice to print out a fresh copy of a ms. rather than to cough up the postage to return it. Your cover letter, if any, can reflect this observation and request the editor to return her comments, either way, in the self-addressed, stamped business-size envelope you have thoughtfully enclosed for that purpose.

As more publishers reluctantly enter the 20th Century (yes, I mean the 20th Century), more are setting the stories they buy from diskettes supplied by the author. They will tell you exactly how they want this done, up to and including how many spaces at the ends of sentences.

Novels, being a different art form, can take a cover page.

Simply use your opening page template, and start your novel with your opening chapter, heading centered, on the next page, at the top, like this:

Chapter One

i

It really was a dark and stormy night. Etc.

#

Note the extra spaces between the chapter header and the small Roman numeral denoting the first scene. This is, to my eye, neater and more attractive than one double space.

It is easier on everybody if you start each new chapter with a new page; some people find it easier for editing if they put each chapter into a separate file. Personally, I keep it all in one big and growing file, which I identify as NOVELNAME_Mtr.doc.

In a Master Document you can do a really universal search and replace, spell-check, etc. This is the document you will print from as well. Also, you don't have to worry about getting the page count all wrong from chapter to chapter as you add or eliminate material.

Do not bind your novel-length ms. for submission; this fairly shrieks, "Amateur!" Send it loose, in a box. Many writers with a penchant for neatness do bind their personal working copies; this writer certainly does.

Most publishers will supply what is called a style sheet--a list of how they do things. A writer who receives such a style sheet is well advised to follow it slavishly. It creates goodwill with the editor because it saves him time and trouble to convert your ms. from the way you do it to the way they do it.

Anticipating the day you do sell your novel and, by some mischance, you draw a copyeditor who wants to write a book--*your* book--here's a useful piece of advice this writer received years ago. Get a small rubber stamp bearing the word "STET" and apply it wherever it seems reasonable to do so, in garish purple ink. Much easier--and makes a bigger statement--than hand writing the instruction.

End

Index

A

Absolute Phrase 106
Adjective 107
Adverb 107
All right 94
Alot 95
Alright 94
Amazing Coincidences 94
antagonist
    forms of 52
Article 108
As You Know Bob 98
Awhile 97

B

black moment
    in plot 52

C

Card Trick in the Dark 99
Case 108
chapter
    first 48
Character building 69
Clause 108
Complement 109
conflict 52
Conjunctions 109
Countersinking 100

Courier Typeface 10
Criticism 80
criticism
    accepting and evaluating 84
critique
    manuscript 70

D

Dangling modifier 99
Deus Ex Machina 101
Different than 96
Disconnected Body Parts 104

E

ellipses 96
Ellipsis 110
Expositional redundancy 100
Eyes 67

F

Fewer 94
Filtration 95

G

gestures
    characteristic or cogitative 61

H

Homophones 97
Hopefully 98
Humor 59

I

Idioms 111
Inflection of adjectives and adverbs
  Comparison 112
Inflection of nouns and pronounsI
  Declension 112
Inflection of verbs
  Conjugation 112
Info dump 98
It's 104

L

Less 94
Lie/lay 122
Literally 91
Little Small Voice (LSV) 64
Lose/loose 101

M

microwriting 12
Modifiers 113, 118
Moods/modes 113
Mystification 93

N

Names
  choosing suitable 104
Nauseous 94
Nearly The Right Word 97
Nouns 114

O

Object 115
Okay 93
Older than 95

P

Passive voice 95, 96, 102, 121
Plot 51
plot
  consruction 51
Point of View 41
Point of View characters
  examples of 44
Predicate 116
Prepositions
  96, 114, 115, 116, 120, 121
Pronoun 117
Pronouns 10, 32, 33, 34, 115, 119
Punctuation
  Apostrophe 32
  Colon
    15, 20, 27, 28, 29, 30, 100
  Comma 20
  Dash 30
  Ellipses 32
  Exclamation Point 19
  Hyphen 29
  Multiple 31
  Parentheses 32
  Period 18
  Question Mark 19
  Quotation Marks 31
  Semi-Colon 27
punctuation, stacked 17

Q

quotation marks
  rules for 15

R

Reader-Cheating 62
resolution of the plot 53

S

Said-Book 20, 36, 38, 96, 100
Sentence 14, 109, 118, 119

setting 51
Setup 47
Show-me 94
Sit /set 122
Speech-tag 100
stacked punctuation 123
style
   personal writing 62

T

Tell-me 94
To cross 103

U

Unique 91

V

Verb 22, 24, 36, 97, 101, 107, 109, 110, 111, 112, 115, 116, 117, 118, 119, 120, 121, 122
Villains 78

W

Weasel-word 98
Workshops 80
workshop
   suggested procedure for 80

About the Author

SASHA MILLER loves teaching so much that it cuts into her writing time. "Maybe," she comments, "there's a message in that somewhere."

She is married to Himself (sometimes referred to as Caesar Augustus), a man even more eccentric than she is, and they are the proud parents of Pandora Josephine Prettypuss Calicat Miller, the Smartest and Sweetest Cat in the Known Universe.

She is the author of eight previous books, including LADYLORD (from TOR), published in 1996. It is a fantasy set in a world reminiscent of medieval Japan. She recently collaborated with Andre Norton on a fantasy trilogy for Tor Books. TO THE KING, A DAUGHTER, published in September, 2000; KNIGHT OR KNAVE , published in June, 2001; and A CROWN DISOWNED, to be published in 2002.

You can contact Sasha Miller at sasha@sff.net. Her website address is http://www.sff.net/people/sasha/.

Illustration of the author by Frank Kelly Freas

About the design

This book was set in a combination of Gowland Overthruster Compressed Ould Gawdy (chosen because is almost precisely resembles Courier without actually being it) and Frammis New Millennium Prayerbook, the latter typeface being based on Wendle Radio Arial Deluxe, designed by Abercrombie V. Wendle, who, to this very day, is dead.

The book was printed on a bunch of mashed-up trees.

Printed in the United States
128869LV00004BA/109/A